# BEST-LOVED
# RECIPES

Publications International, Ltd.

Louis Weber, CEO
Publications International, Ltd.
7373 North Cicero Avenue
Lincolnwood, IL 60712

Permission is never granted for commercial purposes.

**Pictured on the front cover** *(left to right):* Heavenly Ham Roll-Ups *(page 14),* PHILADELPHIA New York-Style Strawberry Swirl Cheesecake *(page 128),* and Potato-Topped Mini Meatloaves *(page 92).*
**Pictured on the back cover** *(left to right):* Chipotle Chicken Bites *(page 8),* PHILLY Buffalo Chicken Dip *(page 58),* and Lemon Tropical Pound Cake *(page 174).*

ISBN: 978-1-4508-8454-9

Library of Congress Control Number: 2012930245

Manufactured in China.

8 7 6 5 4 3 2 1

**Microwave Cooking:** Microwave ovens vary in wattage. Use the cooking times as guidelines and check for doneness before adding more time.

**Preparation/Cooking Times:** Preparation times are based on the approximate amount of time required to assemble the recipe before cooking, baking, chilling, or serving. These times include preparation steps such as measuring, chopping, and mixing. The fact that some preparations and cooking can be done simultaneously is taken into account. Preparation of optional ingredients and serving suggestions is not included.

# Contents

**7**

**72**

**150**

**160**

**67**

# PHILADELPHIA Cream Cheese Tips for the Perfect Cheesecake

For best quality and results, always use PHILADELPHIA Cream Cheese.

**Preheating the oven**—The baking time indicated in a recipe is based on using a preheated oven. Turn the oven on when you start to mix the cheesecake ingredients. This should allow enough time for the oven to heat to the correct temperature for when you are ready to place the cheesecake in the oven to bake. Unless otherwise indicated, always bake cheesecakes in the center of the middle oven rack.

**Beating the batter**—While adding ingredients, do not overbeat the cheesecake batter. Too much air beaten into the batter will result in a cheesecake that sinks in the center when cooled.

**Baking cheesecakes**—Overbaked cheesecakes tend to crack. Remove cheesecake from oven when center is almost set (i.e. center of cheesecake still wiggles when pan is gently shaken from side-to-side). Although the cheesecake appears underbaked, the residual heat in the cheesecake will be enough to finish baking the center. After chilling, the cheesecake will have a perfectly smooth consistency.

**Cooling cheesecakes**—Cool cheesecakes completely before refrigerating. Placing a warm cheesecake in the refrigerator will cause condensation to form on the cake, resulting in a soggy cheesecake.

**Cutting cheesecakes**—Cut cheesecakes when they are cold rather than warm. Use a sharp knife with a clean, thin blade. To make clean cuts, dip the knife in hot water after each cut and wipe the blade clean.

**For all of your occasions, PHILLY MAKES A BETTER CHEESECAKE.**

During tests of plain New York-style cheesecake made with PHILADELPHIA Cream Cheese versus store-brand versions, consumers rated PHILLY cheesecake as better tasting.

KRAFT

PHILADELPHIA

# Appetizers

Best of the best small bites and party starters

# easy-bake cheese & pesto

PREP: 10 min. | TOTAL: 40 min. | MAKES: 12 servings.

## ► what you need!

1 can (4 oz.) reduced-fat refrigerated crescent dinner rolls

1 pkg. (8 oz.) PHILADELPHIA Neufchâtel Cheese

2 Tbsp. pesto

2 Tbsp. chopped roasted red peppers

1 egg, lightly beaten

## ► make it!

1. **HEAT** oven to 350°F.

2. **UNROLL** dough on lightly greased baking sheet; firmly press seams together to form 12×4-inch rectangle.

3. **CUT** cream cheese horizontally in half with sharp knife. Place one of the Neufchâtel pieces on half of dough; top with 1 Tbsp. of the pesto and the peppers. Cover with remaining Neufchâtel piece; spread top with remaining pesto. Brush dough with egg; fold dough in half to completely enclose filling. Press edges of dough together to seal. Brush top with any remaining egg.

4. **BAKE** 15 to 18 min. or until lightly browned. Cool 10 min. Serve with RITZ Reduced Fat Crackers and cut-up fresh vegetables.

   **MAKE AHEAD:**
   Assemble on baking sheet as directed. Cover and refrigerate up to 4 hours. When ready to serve, uncover and bake as directed.

# chipotle chicken bites

PREP: 20 min. | TOTAL: 20 min. | MAKES: 12 servings, 2 topped crackers each.

## ▶ what you need!

2 Tbsp. KRAFT Zesty Italian Dressing

1 small whole chipotle pepper in adobo sauce, chopped

1 cup shredded cooked chicken breast

4 oz. (½ of 8-oz. pkg.) PHILADELPHIA Cream Cheese, softened

½ cup chopped mango

24 RITZ Crackers

2 Tbsp. finely chopped cilantro

## ▶ make it!

1. **PLACE** dressing and chipotle in blender; cover. Blend until smooth. Mix chicken and dressing mixture in small bowl.

2. **MIX** cream cheese and mango in separate small bowl until well blended.

3. **TOP** each cracker with about 1 tsp. cream cheese mixture and about 1 Tbsp. chicken mixture. Sprinkle with cilantro.

**SUBSTITUTE:**
Try cooked pork instead of the chicken.

**SUBSTITUTE:**
Instead of the mango, try fresh raspberries or ripe peaches when in season.

# flavor-infused cream cheese nibbles

PREP: 10 min. | TOTAL: 1 hour 10 min. | MAKES: 18 servings, 2 pieces each.

## ▶ what you need!

1 pkg. (8 oz.) PHILADELPHIA Cream Cheese

½ cup KRAFT Sun-Dried Tomato Dressing

2 cloves garlic, sliced

3 small sprigs fresh rosemary, stems removed

6 sprigs fresh thyme, chopped

1 tsp. black peppercorns

Zest of 1 lemon, cut into thin strips

## ▶ make it!

1. **CUT** cream cheese into 36 pieces; place in pie plate.

2. **ADD** remaining ingredients; mix lightly.

3. **REFRIGERATE** 1 hour. Serve with NABISCO Crackers, crusty bread or pita chips.

**SHORTCUT:**
To simplify, spread softened cream cheese onto bottom of 9-inch pie plate instead of cutting it into pieces. Chop garlic, rosemary, thyme and lemon zest. Mix with dressing and ¼ tsp. ground black pepper; spread over cream cheese. Serve as directed.

**MAKE AHEAD:**
Appetizer can be stored in refrigerator up to 24 hours before serving.

# grilled tomato salsa appetizers

PREP: 15 min. | TOTAL: 25 min. | MAKES: 24 servings, 1 appetizer each.

## ▶ what you need!

12 oz. (about 21) cherry tomatoes

1 small onion, quartered

1 jalapeño pepper

¼ cup KRAFT Zesty Italian Dressing, divided

4 oz. (½ of 8-oz. pkg.) PHILADELPHIA Cream Cheese, softened

2 Tbsp. KRAFT Grated Parmesan Cheese

1 Tbsp. chopped basil

1 French baguette, cut into 24 slices, toasted

## ▶ make it!

1. **HEAT** grill to medium-high heat.

2. **MIX** tomatoes, onion, jalapeño pepper and 2 Tbsp. of the dressing in medium bowl. Mix cream cheese and Parmesan in separate bowl until well blended; set aside.

3. **PLACE** tomatoes and onion on separate skewers. Place skewers and jalapeño pepper on grill grate. Grill 6 to 8 min. or until tender, turning every 2 min. and brushing with remaining 2 Tbsp. dressing.

4. **REMOVE** tomatoes and onion from skewers; chop onion. Seed and chop jalapeño pepper. Mix tomatoes, onion, jalapeño pepper and basil with fork until tomatoes are chunky.

5. **SPREAD** each baguette slice with cream cheese mixture. Top with tomato mixture. Serve warm or cold.

**SUBSTITUTE:**
Prepare as directed, using KRAFT Light Italian Dressing and PHILADELPHIA Neufchâtel Cheese.

**HOW TO HANDLE FRESH CHILE PEPPERS:**
When handling fresh chile peppers, be sure to wear disposable rubber or clear plastic gloves to avoid irritating your skin. Never touch your eyes, nose or mouth when handling the peppers. If you've forgotten to wear the gloves and feel a burning sensation in your hands, apply a baking soda and water paste to the affected area. After rinsing the paste off, you should feel some relief.

# heavenly ham roll-ups

PREP: 15 min. | TOTAL: 35 min. | MAKES: 15 servings.

## ▶ what you need!

1 pkg. (9 oz.) OSCAR MAYER Deli Fresh Shaved Smoked Ham

5 Tbsp. PHILADELPHIA Neufchâtel Cheese

15 fresh asparagus spears (about 1 lb.), trimmed

## ▶ make it!

1. **HEAT** oven to 350°F.

2. **FLATTEN** ham slices; pat dry. Stack ham in piles of 2 slices each; spread each stack with 1 tsp. Neufchâtel.

3. **PLACE** 1 asparagus spear on one long side of each ham stack; roll up. Place, seam-sides down, in 13×9-inch baking dish.

4. **BAKE** 15 to 20 min. or until heated through.

**MAKE AHEAD:**
Assemble roll-ups as directed. Refrigerate up to 24 hours before uncovering and baking as directed.

**SUBSTITUTE:**
Prepare as directed, using 1 package (6 oz.) OSCAR MAYER Thin Sliced Smoked Ham. Substitute 1 slice of ham for every 2 slices of the shaved ham.

# mini cream cheese and pepper jelly phyllo cups

PREP: 20 min. | TOTAL: 40 min. | MAKES: 3 doz. or 12 servings, 3 phyllo cups each.

## ▸ what you need!

6 frozen phyllo sheets, thawed

2 Tbsp. butter, melted

1 pkg. (8 oz.) PHILADELPHIA Cream Cheese, cut into 36 cubes

6 Tbsp. hot pepper jelly

## ▸ make it!

1. **HEAT** oven to 350°F.

2. **BRUSH** 1 phyllo sheet with butter; top with second phyllo sheet. Brush top with butter; cut into 24 (2-inch) squares. Stack 2 squares, on an angle, to make 4 thicknesses; repeat with remaining phyllo sheets and butter. Press 1 stack into each of 36 miniature (1½-inch) muffin cups.

3. **ADD** 1 cream cheese cube to each cup. Bake 20 min. or until cream cheese is melted and pastry is golden brown.

4. **TOP** each serving with ½ tsp. hot pepper jelly.

**SIZE-WISE:**
Select a few of your favorite appetizers rather than sampling one of each to save room for your entrée.

**STORAGE KNOW-HOW:**
Leftover phyllo sheets can be wrapped tightly and refrozen until ready to use.

**MAKE IT EASY:**
Prepare as directed, using purchased jalapeño jelly.

# mini florentine cups

PREP: 20 min. | TOTAL: 35 min. | MAKES: 24 servings.

## ▶ what you need!

1 pkg. (10 oz.) frozen chopped spinach, cooked, well drained

½ cup KRAFT 2% Milk Shredded Mozzarella Cheese

⅓ cup PHILADELPHIA Neufchâtel Cheese

1 Tbsp. KRAFT Grated Parmesan Cheese

1 Tbsp. finely chopped onions

¼ tsp. garlic powder

24 slices OSCAR MAYER Deli Fresh Shaved Oven Roasted Turkey Breast

## ▶ make it!

1. **HEAT** oven to 350°F.

2. **MIX** all ingredients except turkey.

3. **FLATTEN** turkey slices; place 1 slice on bottom and up side of each of 24 miniature (1½-inch) muffin cups. Fill with spinach mixture.

4. **BAKE** 15 min. or until heated through. Cool in pan 5 min. before serving.

**MAKE AHEAD:**
Having a party? Assemble appetizers several hours in advance. Refrigerate until ready to serve. Then, uncover and bake as directed.

**SPECIAL EXTRA:**
Add 1 to 2 Tbsp. chopped water chestnuts to the spinach mixture before spooning into prepared cups.

# mini fruit "pizza"

PREP: 5 min. | TOTAL: 5 min. | MAKES: 1 serving.

## ▶ what you need!

1 CHIPS AHOY! Cookie

1 tsp. PHILADELPHIA Strawberry Cream Cheese Spread

1 tsp. COOL WHIP LITE Whipped Topping (in a can)

1 large strawberry half

## ▶ make it!

**TOP** cookie with remaining ingredients.

**VARIATION:**
Prepare using your favorite varieties of PHILADELPHIA Cream Cheese Spread and fruit.

# mini new potato bites

## ▶ what you need!

15  new potatoes (1½ lb.)

 4  oz. (½ of 8-oz. pkg.) PHILADELPHIA Cream Cheese, softened

 2  Tbsp. BREAKSTONE'S or KNUDSEN Sour Cream

 2  Tbsp. KRAFT Grated Parmesan Cheese

 4  slices OSCAR MAYER Bacon, cooked, crumbled

 2  Tbsp. chopped fresh chives

## ▶ make it!

1. **COOK** potatoes in boiling water in large saucepan 15 min. or until tender.

2. **MEANWHILE,** mix cream cheese, sour cream and Parmesan. Refrigerate until ready to use.

3. **DRAIN** potatoes. Cool slightly. Cut in half, then cut small piece from rounded bottom of each. Place, bottom-sides down, on platter; top with cream cheese mixture, bacon and chives.

**MAKE AHEAD:**
These potatoes are delicious served hot or cold.

**SPECIAL EXTRA:**
For added flavor, prepare using ½ cup PHILADELPHIA Chive & Onion Cream Cheese Spread.

# mini shrimp cocktail bites

PREP: 10 min. | TOTAL: 10 min. | MAKES: 8 servings, 2 topped crackers each.

## ▶ what you need!

16  RITZ or Holiday RITZ Crackers

⅓  cup PHILADELPHIA Whipped Cream Cheese Spread

⅓  cup KRAFT Cocktail Sauce

16  cleaned large fresh shrimp, cooked

⅓  cup finely chopped green onions

## ▶ make it!

1. **SPREAD** each cracker with 1 tsp. of the cream cheese spread.

2. **TOP** evenly with the cocktail sauce, shrimp and onions.

**KEEPING IT SAFE:**
Frozen shrimp can also be used to prepare these appetizers. To thaw the shrimp, place the bag of frozen shrimp in the refrigerator and let stand until thawed. Or, place the sealed bag of shrimp in a bowl of cold water and let stand until thawed, changing the water every 10 min. Never thaw the shrimp on the countertop.

# savory parmesan bites

PREP: 15 min. | TOTAL: 30 min. | MAKES: 32 servings.

## ▶ what you need!

1 pkg. (8 oz.) PHILADELPHIA Cream Cheese, softened

1 cup KRAFT Grated Parmesan Cheese, divided

2 cans (8 oz. each) refrigerated crescent dinner rolls

1 cup chopped red peppers

¼ cup chopped fresh parsley

## ▶ make it!

1. **HEAT** oven to 350°F.

2. **BEAT** cream cheese and ¾ cup Parmesan with mixer until well blended.

3. **SEPARATE** crescent rolls into 8 rectangles; press perforations together to seal. Spread each with 3 Tbsp. cream cheese mixture. Top with peppers and parsley. Fold one long side of each dough rectangle over filling to center; fold again to enclose filling. Cut each into 4 squares. Place, seam-sides down, on baking sheet. Sprinkle with remaining Parmesan.

4. **BAKE** 13 to 15 min. or until golden brown.

**SIZE-WISE:**
At your next party, select a few of your favorite appetizers rather than sampling one of each to save room for your entrée.

**SUBSTITUTE:**
Substitute 1 jar (12 oz.) roasted red peppers, drained and chopped, for the red peppers.

**VARIATION:**
Substitute 1 jar (13¼ oz.) sliced mushrooms or 1 package (3 oz.) pepperoni slices for the red peppers and parsley.

# shrimp pizza squares

**PREP: 10 min. | TOTAL: 35 min. | MAKES: 36 servings.**

## ▶ what you need!

1 can (13.8 oz.) refrigerated pizza crust

1 lb. uncooked deveined peeled medium shrimp

3 cloves garlic, minced

2 Tbsp. KRAFT Zesty Italian Dressing

4 oz. (½ of 8-oz. pkg.) PHILADELPHIA Cream Cheese, softened

1 cup KRAFT Shredded Italian Mozzarella-Parmesan Cheese Blend*

1 cup roasted red pepper strips

¼ cup chopped fresh basil

*Made with quality cheeses crafted in the USA.*

## ▶ make it!

1. **HEAT** oven to 425°F.

2. **UNROLL** dough onto baking sheet sprayed lightly with cooking spray; press into 13×9-inch rectangle. Bake 12 to 15 min. or until lightly browned.

3. **MEANWHILE,** cook shrimp and garlic in dressing in large skillet on medium-high heat 3 to 5 min. or until shrimp turn pink, stirring frequently. Remove from heat; drain.

4. **SPREAD** cream cheese onto pizza crust, leaving ¼-inch border around sides. Top with shrimp, shredded cheese and peppers. Bake 10 min. or until shredded cheese is melted. Sprinkle with basil.

**SUBSTITUTE:**
For variety, top pizza with sliced fresh mushrooms and/or chopped artichoke hearts instead of the roasted peppers.

**SPECIAL EXTRA:**
Sprinkle pizza with ½ tsp. crushed red pepper, or more to taste, before baking as directed.

# spring veggie pizza appetizer

PREP: 20 min. | TOTAL: 2 hours 35 min. | MAKES: 32 servings.

## ▶ what you need!

2 pkg. (8 oz. each) refrigerated crescent dinner rolls

1 tub (8 oz.) PHILADELPHIA Cream Cheese Spread

½ cup MIRACLE WHIP Dressing

1 tsp. dill weed

½ tsp. onion salt

1 cup each chopped sugar snap peas and quartered cherry tomatoes

½ cup each sliced radishes, chopped yellow peppers and shredded carrots

3 green onions, chopped

## ▶ make it!

1. **HEAT** oven to 375°F.

2. **UNROLL** dough; separate into 4 rectangles. Press onto bottom and up sides of 15×10×1-inch pan, firmly pressing seams and perforations together to seal.

3. **BAKE** 11 to 13 min. or until golden brown; cool.

4. **MIX** cream cheese spread, dressing, dill weed and onion salt until well blended; spread onto crust. Top with remaining ingredients. Refrigerate 2 hours.

**SUBSTITUTE:**
Substitute chopped cucumbers and/or chopped red peppers for any of the chopped vegetables.

# zesty stuffed olives

PREP: 10 min. | TOTAL: 10 min. | MAKES: about 2 doz. or 11 servings, about 2 stuffed olives each.

## ▸ what you need!

½ cup PHILADELPHIA Cream Cheese Spread

1 can (5.75 oz.) colossal black olives, drained

2 Tbsp. KRAFT Zesty Italian Dressing

2 Tbsp. chopped fresh parsley

## ▸ make it!

1. **SPOON** cream cheese spread into small resealable plastic bag. Press cream cheese into one of the bottom corners of bag. Cut off small piece from corner of bag. Squeeze cream cheese into centers of olives.

2. **PLACE** olives on serving plate. Drizzle with dressing. Sprinkle with parsley.

   **SUBSTITUTE:**
   Prepare as directed, using PHILADELPHIA Chive & Onion Cream Cheese Spread.

# sweet pepper-ham wraps

PREP: 10 min. | TOTAL: 10 min. | MAKES: 1 doz. or 4 servings, 3 wrapped peppers each.

## ▶ what you need!

1 each red and green pepper

2 Tbsp. PHILADELPHIA Neufchâtel Cheese, softened

12 slices OSCAR MAYER Deli Fresh Shaved Smoked Ham

## ▶ make it!

1. **CUT** peppers lengthwise in half; remove and discard seeds. Cut each piece into 3 lengthwise strips.

2. **DRY** insides with paper towel; spread evenly with Neufchâtel.

3. **PLACE** 1 pepper strip on each ham slice; wrap ham around pepper. Secure with wooden toothpicks.

**SUBSTITUTE:**
Substitute OSCAR MAYER Light Bologna for the ham.

**MAKE AHEAD:**
Wraps can be stored, tightly covered, in refrigerator up to 2 days.

# cream cheese-bacon crescents

PREP: 15 min. | TOTAL: 30 min. | MAKES: 16 servings.

## ▶ what you need!

1 tub (8 oz.) PHILADELPHIA Chive & Onion Cream Cheese Spread

3 slices OSCAR MAYER Bacon, cooked, crumbled

2 cans (8 oz. each) refrigerated crescent dinner rolls

## ▶ make it!

1. **HEAT** oven to 375°F.

2. **MIX** cream cheese spread and bacon until well blended.

3. **SEPARATE** each can of dough into 8 triangles. Cut each triangle lengthwise in half. Spread each dough triangle with 1 generous tsp. cream cheese mixture. Roll up, starting at shortest side of triangle; place, point-sides down, on baking sheet.

4. **BAKE** 12 to 15 min. or until golden brown. Serve warm.

**VARIATION:**
For a sweet version, prepare using PHILADELPHIA Strawberry Cream Cheese Spread and substituting chopped PLANTERS Walnuts for the bacon.

# blueberry cracker bites

**PREP: 5 min. | TOTAL: 5 min. | MAKES: 1 serving.**

## ► what you need!

2  RITZ Reduced Fat Crackers

2  tsp. PHILADELPHIA Neufchâtel Cheese

10  frozen blueberries

## ► make it!

**1.** **SPREAD** crackers with Neufchâtel.

**2.** **TOP** with berries.

**SUBSTITUTE:**
Substitute 4 frozen raspberries for the blueberries.

# Dips & Spreads

Our hot, cold, sweet, and savory favorites

# baked apricot spread

## ▶ what you need!

1 pkg. (8 oz.) PHILADELPHIA Cream Cheese, softened

1 cup KRAFT Shredded Cheddar Cheese

½ cup BREAKSTONE'S or KNUDSEN Sour Cream

½ cup sliced dried apricots

⅓ cup PLANTERS Sliced Almonds

RITZ Crackers

## ▶ make it!

1. **HEAT** oven to 350°F.

2. **MIX** cream cheese and Cheddar in medium bowl until well blended. Add sour cream and apricots; mix well.

3. **SPREAD** into 9-inch pie plate; sprinkle with nuts.

4. **BAKE** 25 to 30 min. or until nuts are lightly toasted and spread is heated through. Cool slightly. Serve with crackers.

**SERVING SUGGESTION:**
Enjoy the fruit and cheese flavors of this spread, but watch your portion size.

**SPECIAL EXTRA:**
For a spicier spread, add 2 Tbsp. mango chutney to the cream cheese mixture before spreading into pie plate.

# apple, pecan &
# blue cheese spread

PREP: 10 min. | TOTAL: 2 hours 10 min. | MAKES: 3 cups or 24 servings, 2 Tbsp. spread and 6 crackers each.

## ▶ what you need!

1 container (8 oz.) PHILADELPHIA Light Cream Cheese Spread

½ cup BREAKSTONE'S Reduced Fat or KNUDSEN Light Sour Cream

1 Rome Beauty apple, finely chopped

¼ cup ATHENOS Crumbled Blue Cheese

¼ cup chopped red onion

¼ cup chopped toasted PLANTERS Pecans

TRISCUIT Crackers

## ▶ make it!

1. **BEAT** cream cheese spread and sour cream in medium bowl until well blended.

2. **ADD** apples, blue cheese, onions and nuts; mix well. Cover.

3. **REFRIGERATE** at least 2 hours. Serve as a spread with the crackers.

**SERVING SUGGESTION:**
For a unique dip container, cut top off and hollow out a large red apple. Stand upright on serving platter and fill with dip just before serving. Surround with crackers.

# layered sun-dried tomato and artichoke spread

PREP: 10 min. | TOTAL: 1 hour 10 min. | MAKES: 12 servings, 2 Tbsp. spread and 5 RITZ crackers each.

## ▶ what you need!

1 pkg. (8 oz.) PHILADELPHIA Cream Cheese, well chilled

3 Tbsp. finely chopped sun-dried tomatoes in oil, well drained

3 Tbsp. finely chopped drained canned artichoke hearts

2 Tbsp. pesto

2 Tbsp. chopped PLANTERS Smoked Almonds

2 tsp. chopped fresh parsley

RITZ Crackers, WHEAT THINS Big Snacks and TRISCUIT Crackers

## ▶ make it!

1. **CUT** cream cheese horizontally into 3 slices. (See Tip.) Place 1 slice on large sheet of plastic wrap; top with tomatoes and second cream cheese slice.

2. **COMBINE** artichokes and pesto; spoon over second cream cheese layer.

3. **TOP** with remaining cream cheese slice, nuts and parsley; press nuts and parsley lightly into cream cheese to secure. Wrap with plastic wrap. Refrigerate 1 hour. Serve with RITZ crackers, WHEAT THINS Big and TRISCUIT crackers.

**HOW TO CUT CREAM CHEESE WITH DENTAL FLOSS:**
Wrap 18-inch piece of dental floss around bottom third of cream cheese brick, overlapping ends. Pull ends steadily to cut cream cheese. Repeat to make a total of 3 slices.

# easy layered tomato dip

PREP: 10 min. | TOTAL: 3 hours 10 min. | MAKES: 3 cups dip or 24 servings, 2 Tbsp. dip and 16 crackers each.

## ▸ what you need!

1 pkg. (8 oz.) PHILADELPHIA Neufchâtel Cheese, softened

2 cloves garlic, minced

2 small tomatoes, chopped

3 green onions, sliced

¼ cup KRAFT 2% Milk Shredded Cheddar Cheese

WHEAT THINS Reduced Fat Baked Snack Crackers

## ▸ make it!

1. **MIX** Neufchâtel and garlic until well blended.

2. **SPREAD** onto bottom of shallow serving bowl or 9-inch pie plate; top with tomatoes, onions and Cheddar. Refrigerate 3 hours or until chilled.

3. **SERVE** with crackers.

**SUBSTITUTE:**
Prepare using WHEAT THINS Multi-Grain Snack Crackers.

# fiesta baked cheese dip

PREP: 20 min. | TOTAL: 40 min. | MAKES: 4 cups or 32 servings, 2 Tbsp. each.

## ▶ what you need!

2 pkg. (8 oz. each) PHILADELPHIA Cream Cheese, softened

1 pkg. (8 oz.) KRAFT Mexican Style Finely Shredded Four Cheese, divided

1 can (4 oz.) chopped green chiles, undrained

1¼ cups BREAKSTONE'S or KNUDSEN Sour Cream, divided

¼ to ½ tsp. ground red pepper (cayenne)

## ▶ make it!

1. **HEAT** oven to 350°F.

2. **BEAT** cream cheese in large bowl with mixer until creamy. Reserve ¼ cup shredded cheese. Add remaining shredded cheese to cream cheese with chiles, ½ cup sour cream and ground red pepper; mix well.

3. **SPOON** into 10-inch pie plate or quiche dish.

4. **BAKE** 20 min. or until edge is lightly browned. Top with remaining sour cream and shredded cheese. Serve with tortilla chips.

**SUBSTITUTE:**
Substitute KRAFT Shredded Colby & Monterey Jack Cheese for Mexican Style Shredded Cheese.

**SPECIAL EXTRA:**
Assemble dip and bake as directed. Top with 2 Tbsp. chopped green onions or chopped fresh cilantro.

# greek antipasto dip

PREP: 10 min. | TOTAL: 22 min. | MAKES: 2 cups dip or 16 servings, 2 Tbsp. dip and 16 crackers each.

## ▶ what you need!

1 pkg. (8 oz.) PHILADELPHIA Neufchâtel Cheese, softened

1 clove garlic, finely chopped

⅓ cup chopped roasted red peppers

¼ cup finely chopped red onions

1 Tbsp. olive oil

¼ cup ATHENOS Crumbled Reduced Fat Feta Cheese

½ small lemon, seeded

1 Tbsp. minced fresh parsley

WHEAT THINS Original Snacks

## ▶ make it!

1. **HEAT** oven to 350°F.

2. **MIX** Neufchâtel and garlic; spread onto bottom of 9-inch pie plate.

3. **COVER** with peppers and onions. Drizzle with oil; sprinkle with feta cheese.

4. **BAKE** 10 to 12 min. or until heated through. Squeeze lemon over dip. Sprinkle with parsley. Serve with WHEAT THINS.

**SERVING SUGGESTION:**
Serve with WHEAT THINS Big Snack Crackers.

# hot apple pie dip

PREP: 10 min. | TOTAL: 22 min. | MAKES: 2 cups or 16 servings, 2 Tbsp. dip and 15 crackers each.

## ▶ what you need!

1 tub (8 oz.) PHILADELPHIA Light Cream Cheese Spread

2 Tbsp. packed brown sugar

½ tsp. pumpkin pie spice

1 apple, chopped, divided

¼ cup KRAFT 2% Milk Shredded Reduced Fat Cheddar Cheese

1 Tbsp. finely chopped PLANTERS Pecan Pieces

WHEAT THINS Lightly Cinnamon Snack Crackers

## ▶ make it!

1. **HEAT** oven to 375°F.

2. **MIX** cream cheese spread, sugar and spice in medium bowl until well blended. Stir in half of the chopped apple.

3. **SPREAD** into 8-inch pie plate or small casserole dish. Top with remaining apples, Cheddar and nuts.

4. **BAKE** 10 to 12 min. or until heated through. Serve with the crackers.

**SUBSTITUTE:**
Substitute ground cinnamon for the pumpkin pie spice.

# layered pesto and red pepper dip

PREP: 15 min. | TOTAL: 1 hour 15 min. | MAKES: about 1 cup or 9 servings, 2 Tbsp. dip and 16 crackers each.

## ▶ what you need!

1 tub (8 oz.) PHILADELPHIA Light Cream Cheese Spread, divided

¼ cup chopped drained roasted red peppers

1 Tbsp. pesto

1 Tbsp. milk

WHEAT THINS Original Snacks

## ▶ make it!

1. **PLACE** half of the cream cheese spread and the peppers in blender; cover. Blend 30 to 40 sec. or until well blended, stopping and scraping down side of blender as needed.

2. **MIX** remaining cream cheese spread, pesto and milk until well blended. Spread onto small serving plate; top with the red pepper mixture. Cover.

3. **REFRIGERATE** at least 1 hour before serving. Serve with WHEAT THINS.

**MAKE AHEAD:**
The two layers of dip can be made up to 1 day ahead and stored in separate tightly covered containers in the refrigerator. For best results, layer the dips no more than 2 hours before serving.

# nut and honey pear dip

PREP: 5 min. | TOTAL: 7 min. | MAKES: 16 servings, 2 Tbsp. dip and 5 crackers each.

## ▸ what you need!

½ cup PLANTERS Walnut Pieces

¼ cup honey, divided

1 pkg. (8 oz.) PHILADELPHIA Neufchâtel Cheese, softened

1 medium pear, chopped

RITZ Reduced Fat Crackers

## ▸ make it!

1. **MIX** nuts and 2 Tbsp. of the honey in small bowl; set aside.

2. **COMBINE** Neufchâtel, remaining 2 Tbsp. honey and pear in medium bowl until well blended. Spread mixture onto bottom of microwaveable dish or 9-inch pie plate. Top with nut mixture.

3. **MICROWAVE** on HIGH 1 to 2 min. or until heated through. Serve with crackers.

**STORAGE KNOW-HOW:**
Nuts have a high oil content that makes them susceptible to spoilage. To keep shelled nuts from turning rancid, store them in the refrigerator. If you buy nuts in bulk and want to keep them for several months, store them in the freezer.

# PHILADELPHIA tuscan dip

**PREP:** 10 min. | **TOTAL:** 1 hour 10 min. | **MAKES:** 1½ cups or 12 servings, 2 Tbsp. each.

## ▶ what you need!

1 pkg. (8 oz.) PHILADELPHIA Cream Cheese, softened

2 Tbsp. BREAKSTONE'S or KNUDSEN Sour Cream

½ cup finely chopped sun-dried tomatoes

½ cup chopped black olives

¼ cup finely chopped red onions

WHEAT THINS Original Snacks

## ▶ make it!

**1. MIX** cream cheese and sour cream in medium bowl until well blended.

**2. ADD** all remaining ingredients except crackers; mix well.

**3. REFRIGERATE** 1 hour. Serve with WHEAT THINS.

**SERVING SUGGESTION:**
Serve with cut-up fresh vegetables in addition to/instead of the crackers.

**HOW TO HYDRATE SUN-DRIED TOMATOES:**
Place tomatoes in small bowl; pour boiling water over tomatoes to cover. Let stand 5 to 10 min. to soften tomatoes. Drain; pat dry.

# PHILLY buffalo chicken dip

PREP: 10 min. | TOTAL: 12 min. | MAKES: 2¼ cups or 18 servings, 2 Tbsp. each.

## ▸ what you need!

1 pkg. (8 oz.) PHILADELPHIA Cream Cheese, softened

1 pkg. (6 oz.) OSCAR MAYER Oven Roasted Chicken Breast Cuts

½ cup Buffalo wing sauce

¼ cup KRAFT Natural Blue Cheese Crumbles

¼ cup sliced green onions

## ▸ make it!

1. **SPREAD** cream cheese onto bottom of microwaveable 9-inch pie plate. Mix chicken and sauce; spoon over cream cheese. Sprinkle with blue cheese and onions.

2. **MICROWAVE** on HIGH 2 min. or until heated through.

3. **SERVE** warm with celery sticks and WHEAT THINS Original Snacks.

# spiced cranberry dip

PREP: 10 min. | TOTAL: 10 min. | MAKES: 1¾ cups or 14 servings, 2 Tbsp. each.

## ▶ what you need!

1 pkg. (8 oz.) PHILADELPHIA Cream Cheese, softened

½ cup canned whole berry cranberry sauce

¼ cup orange marmalade

⅛ tsp. ground red pepper (cayenne)

¼ cup PLANTERS Slivered Almonds, toasted

## ▶ make it!

1. **SPREAD** cream cheese onto bottom of 9-inch pie plate.

2. **MIX** next 3 ingredients; spoon over cream cheese. Top with nuts.

3. **SERVE** with RITZ Crackers.

**VARIATION:**
Prepare as directed, omitting the red pepper and substituting hot pepper jelly for the orange marmalade.

# PHILLY cheesy chili dip

**PREP: 5 min. | TOTAL: 6 min. | MAKES: 3 cups or 24 servings, 2 Tbsp. each.**

## ▶ what you need!

1  pkg. (8 oz.) PHILADELPHIA Cream Cheese, softened

1  can (15 oz.) chili

½  cup KRAFT Shredded Cheddar Cheese

2  Tbsp. chopped fresh cilantro

## ▶ make it!

1. **SPREAD** cream cheese onto bottom of microwaveable 9-inch pie plate; top with chili and Cheddar.

2. **MICROWAVE** on HIGH 45 sec. to 1 min. or until Cheddar is melted; sprinkle with cilantro.

3. **SERVE** with assorted NABISCO Crackers and cut-up fresh vegetables.

**SERVE AS A TOPPER:**
Place unwrapped block of cream cheese on microwaveable plate; top with chili and Cheddar. Then, microwave and garnish with cilantro before serving as directed.

**NOTE:**
Use your favorite variety of canned chili—with or without beans, regular or spicy.

# sun-dried tomato & garlic dip

PREP: 5 min. | TOTAL: 5 min. | MAKES: 2 cups or 16 servings, 2 Tbsp. each.

## ▶ what you need!

1 tub (8 oz.) PHILADELPHIA Cream Cheese Spread

½ cup MIRACLE WHIP Dressing

½ cup sun-dried tomatoes packed in oil, drained, chopped

2 Tbsp. finely chopped fresh chives

1 clove garlic, minced

1 tsp. black pepper

## ▶ make it!

1. **MIX** all ingredients until well blended.

2. **SERVE** with cut-up fresh vegetables or NABISCO Crackers, if desired.

**MAKE AHEAD:**
This dip can be made up to 24 hours in advance. The longer you leave this dip in the refrigerator, the better the flavor.

# warm reuben spread

**PREP:** 15 min. | **TOTAL:** 35 min. | **MAKES:** 2½ cups spread or 20 servings, 2 Tbsp. spread and 6 crackers.

## ▶ what you need!

4 oz. (½ of 8-oz. pkg.) PHILADELPHIA Cream Cheese, softened

½ cup KRAFT Thousand Island Dressing

¼ lb. sliced deli corned beef, chopped (about 1 cup)

¾ cup well-drained CLAUSSEN Sauerkraut

1 pkg. (8 oz.) KRAFT Big Slice Swiss Cheese Slices, chopped

TRISCUIT Deli-Style Rye Crackers

## ▶ make it!

1. **HEAT** oven to 350°F.

2. **MIX** cream cheese and dressing in medium bowl; stir in all remaining ingredients except crackers.

3. **SPREAD** onto bottom of 9-inch pie plate or shallow dish.

4. **BAKE** 20 min. or until heated through. Serve warm with crackers.

**USE YOUR MICROWAVE:**
Instead of baking the prepared spread, microwave it instead. Assemble dip as directed in shallow microwaveable dish. Microwave on HIGH 2 to 3 min. or until heated through. Serve as directed.

**SUBSTITUTE:**
Prepare using TRISCUIT Thin Crisps.

# baked triple-veggie dip

**PREP: 15 min. | TOTAL: 50 min. | MAKES: 4½ cups or 36 servings, 2 Tbsp. each.**

## ▶ what you need!

1½ cups KRAFT Grated Parmesan Cheese, divided

1 can (1 lb. 3 oz.) asparagus spears, drained, chopped

1 pkg. (10 oz.) frozen chopped spinach, thawed, drained

1 can (8½ oz.) artichoke hearts, drained, chopped

1 container (8 oz.) PHILADELPHIA Chive & Onion Cream Cheese Spread

½ cup KRAFT Real Mayo Mayonnaise

## ▶ make it!

1. **HEAT** oven to 375°F.

2. **MIX** 1¼ cups Parmesan with all remaining ingredients.

3. **SPOON** into 2-qt. baking dish; top with remaining Parmesan.

4. **BAKE** 35 min. or until dip is heated through and top is lightly browned.

**VARIATION:**
Prepare as directed, using KRAFT Reduced Fat Parmesan Style Grated Topping, PHILADELPHIA Chive & Onion ⅓ Less Fat than Cream Cheese and KRAFT Mayo with Olive Oil Reduced Fat Mayonnaise.

**NUTRITION BONUS:**
The spinach is a good source of vitamin A in this tasty baked dip.

# citrus & herb-cream cheese spread

PREP: 10 min. | TOTAL: 10 min. | MAKES: 12 servings, 3 topped crackers each.

## ▶ what you need!

36 TRISCUIT Crackers

¾ cup PHILADELPHIA Chive & Onion ⅓ Less Fat than Cream Cheese

1 Tbsp. orange marmalade

1 Tbsp. chopped fresh chives

## ▶ make it!

**1.** **SPREAD** crackers with cream cheese.

**2.** **TOP** with marmalade and chives.

# Entrées & Sides

Crowd-pleasing casseroles, pasta, and accompaniments

# creamy zucchini
# & spinach rigatoni

**PREP: 20 min. | TOTAL: 45 min. | MAKES: 6 servings, 1⅓ cups each.**

## ▶ what you need!

8 oz. (½ of 16-oz. pkg.) rigatoni pasta, uncooked

1 tsp. oil

1 zucchini, sliced

½ lb. sliced fresh mushrooms

2 cloves garlic, minced

1 Tbsp. flour

¼ tsp. each dried basil leaves, oregano leaves and crushed red pepper

1 cup fat-free reduced-sodium chicken broth

4 oz. (½ of 8-oz. pkg.) PHILADELPHIA Neufchâtel Cheese, cubed

1 pkg. (6 oz.) baby spinach leaves

¼ cup KRAFT Grated Parmesan Cheese

1½ cups KRAFT Shredded Mozzarella Cheese with a Touch of PHILADELPHIA, divided

## ▶ make it!

1. **HEAT** oven to 375°F.

2. **COOK** pasta in large saucepan as directed on package, omitting salt.

3. **MEANWHILE,** heat oil in large skillet on medium heat. Add zucchini, mushrooms and garlic; cook and stir 3 to 4 min. or until zucchini is crisp-tender. Add flour and seasonings; cook and stir 1 min. Stir in broth; cook and stir 2 to 3 min. or until thickened. Add Neufchâtel; cook and stir 2 to 3 min. or until melted.

4. **DRAIN** pasta; return to pan. Add zucchini mixture, spinach, Parmesan and ½ cup mozzarella; mix lightly. Spoon into 2-qt. casserole sprayed with cooking spray; top with remaining mozzarella.

5. **BAKE** 10 min. or until mozzarella is melted.

**SERVING SUGGESTION:**
Serve with fresh fruit and a side salad to round out the meal.

# 20-minute skillet salmon

PREP: 10 min. | TOTAL: 20 min. | MAKES: 4 servings.

## ▶ what you need!

1 Tbsp. oil

4 salmon fillets (1 lb.)

1 cup fat-free milk

½ cup (½ of 8-oz. tub) PHILADELPHIA Neufchâtel Cheese

½ cup chopped cucumbers

2 Tbsp. chopped fresh dill

## ▶ make it!

1. **HEAT** oil in large skillet on medium-high heat.

2. **ADD** salmon; cook 5 min. on each side or until salmon flakes easily with fork. Remove from skillet; cover to keep warm.

3. **ADD** milk and Neufchâtel to skillet; cook and stir until smooth. Stir in cucumbers and dill.

4. **RETURN** salmon to skillet. Cook 2 min. or until heated through. Serve topped with Neufchâtel sauce.

**SERVING SUGGESTION:**
Round out the meal with hot cooked rice and steamed vegetables. Or serve salmon on a bed of salad greens.

**COOKING KNOW-HOW:**
When salmon is done, it will appear opaque and flake easily with fork.

**FOOD FACTS:**
Check salmon fillets for bones before cooking by running fingers over surface. Small bumps are usually a sign of bones—use tweezers to remove them.

**SUBSTITUTE:**
Substitute 2 tsp. dill weed for the 2 Tbsp. chopped fresh dill.

# bruschetta & ham sandwich

**PREP: 10 min. | TOTAL: 10 min. | MAKES: 2 servings, 1 sandwich each.**

## ▶ what you need!

½ cup chopped tomatoes

1 Tbsp. chopped fresh basil

1 Tbsp. KRAFT Reduced Fat Parmesan Style Grated Topping

1 Tbsp. KRAFT Light Zesty Italian Dressing

2 whole wheat panini sandwich buns (6 inch), partially split

2 Tbsp. PHILADELPHIA Neufchâtel Cheese

2 romaine lettuce leaves

12 slices OSCAR MAYER Deli Fresh Shaved Smoked Ham

## ▶ make it!

1. **COMBINE** first 4 ingredients.

2. **SPREAD** bottom halves of buns with Neufchâtel.

3. **FILL** with lettuce, ham and tomato mixture.

**SUBSTITUTE:**
Prepare using OSCAR MAYER Deli Fresh Shaved Oven Roasted Turkey Breast or Rotisserie Seasoned Chicken Breast.

**SHORTCUT:**
Don't have fresh basil? You can use 1 tsp. dried basil leaves instead.

**MAKE AHEAD:**
Sandwiches can be made ahead of time. Wrap individually in plastic wrap. Refrigerate up to 24 hours before serving.

# enchiladas suizas

PREP: 25 min. | TOTAL: 45 min. | MAKES: 6 servings, 2 enchiladas each.

## ▶ what you need!

1 pkg. (8 oz.) PHILADELPHIA Cream Cheese, softened, divided

½ cup sliced green onions

1 cup KRAFT Shredded Sharp Cheddar Cheese

1 cup KRAFT Shredded Monterey Jack Cheese

2 cans (4 oz. each) chopped green chiles, drained

½ tsp. ground cumin

3 eggs

1 Tbsp. oil

12 corn tortillas

2 jars (8 oz. each) enchilada sauce

1 can (4¼ oz.) sliced black olives, drained

## ▶ make it!

1. **HEAT** oven to 350°F.

2. **PLACE** half of the cream cheese and the onions in small bowl. Beat with electric mixer on medium speed until well blended; set aside for later use.

3. **PLACE** remaining cream cheese, Cheddar, Monterey Jack, green chiles and cumin in large bowl. Beat with electric mixer on medium speed until well blended. Add eggs, 1 at a time, beating well after each addition; set aside. Heat oil in medium skillet. Add tortillas; cook just until warmed. Spoon 2 Tbsp. of the cheese mixture onto each tortilla; roll up. Place, seam-sides down, in 13×9-inch baking dish; top with the enchilada sauce.

4. **BAKE** 20 min. or until heated through. Top with the reserved cream cheese mixture and the olives.

**SERVING SUGGESTION:**
Serve with a mixed green salad for added color and texture.

**SUBSTITUTE:**
Substitute PHILADELPHIA Neufchâtel Cheese for the cream cheese.

# corn souffle

PREP: 15 min. | TOTAL: 55 min. | MAKES: 16 servings.

## ► what you need!

2  Tbsp. butter

1  pkg. (8 oz.) PHILADELPHIA Cream Cheese, cubed

1  can (15¼ oz.) whole kernel corn, drained

1  can (14.75 oz.) cream-style corn

1  pkg. (8.5 oz.) corn muffin mix

2  eggs, lightly beaten

1  cup KRAFT Shredded Cheddar Cheese

## ► make it!

1. **HEAT** oven to 350°F.

2. **MICROWAVE** butter in medium microwaveable bowl on HIGH 30 sec. or until melted. Add cream cheese; continue microwaving 15 sec. or until cream cheese is softened; stir until well blended. Add both corns, muffin mix and eggs; mix well.

3. **POUR** into greased 13×9-inch baking pan; sprinkle with Cheddar.

4. **BAKE** 40 min. or until golden brown. Cool slightly.

**SERVING SUGGESTION:**
This dish is versatile enough to pair with your favorite barbecued meat, beef stew, chicken soup or even chili.

**VARIATION:**
**Mexican-Style Corn Souffle:** Prepare as directed, using 1 can (11 oz.) whole kernel corn with chopped red and green peppers.

**SPECIAL EXTRA:**
Add ¼ cup sliced green onions along with the corn, muffin mix and eggs.

# creamed corn

PREP: 5 min. | TOTAL: 10 min. | MAKES: 6 servings, ½ cup each.

## ▶ what you need!

2 oz. (¼ of 8-oz. pkg.) PHILADELPHIA Cream Cheese, cubed

2 Tbsp. milk

1 can (14.75 oz.) cream-style corn

1 pkg. (10 oz.) frozen corn, thawed

½ cup KRAFT Shredded Sharp Cheddar Cheese

⅓ cup sliced green onions

## ▶ make it!

1. **COOK** cream cheese and milk in medium saucepan on medium heat until cream cheese is melted, stirring frequently.

2. **STIR** in corns; cook 4 min. or until heated through, stirring occasionally.

3. **SPOON** into serving dish; sprinkle with Cheddar and onions.

**SPECIAL EXTRA:**
Stir in a dash or two of hot pepper sauce.

# cheesy chicken tostadas

PREP: 10 min. | TOTAL: 17 min. | MAKES: 6 servings, 1 tostada each.

## ▶ what you need!

6  tostada shells

½  cup PHILADELPHIA Chive & Onion Cream Cheese Spread

¾  lb. cooked chicken, shredded

6  KRAFT Singles

1  avocado, sliced

1½  cups shredded lettuce

1  medium tomato, chopped

## ▶ make it!

1. **HEAT** oven to 375°F.

2. **SPREAD** tostada shells evenly with cream cheese spread; place on baking sheet. Fill evenly with chicken and Singles.

3. **BAKE** 5 to 7 min. or until heated through.

4. **TOP** with the avocados, lettuce and tomatoes.

**SUBSTITUTE:**
Substitute shredded cooked beef or pork for the chicken.

# creamy vegetable bake

PREP: 20 min. | TOTAL: 50 min. | MAKES: 10 servings, ¾ cup each.

## ▶ what you need!

1 pkg. (8 oz.) PHILADELPHIA Cream Cheese, softened

⅓ cup milk

¼ cup KRAFT Grated Parmesan Cheese

1 tsp. dried basil leaves

4 large carrots, diagonally sliced

½ lb. sugar snap peas

½ lb. fresh asparagus, cut into 1-inch lengths

1 large red pepper, chopped

1 pkg. (6 oz.) STOVE TOP Stuffing Mix for Chicken

## ▶ make it!

1. **HEAT** oven to 350°F.

2. **MICROWAVE** cream cheese and milk in large microwaveable bowl on HIGH 1 min. or until cream cheese is melted and mixture is blended when stirred. Add Parmesan and basil; stir until blended. Add vegetables; toss to coat.

3. **SPOON** into greased 13×9-inch baking dish. Prepare stuffing as directed on package; spoon over vegetable mixture.

4. **BAKE** 30 min. or until golden brown.

**SUBSTITUTE:**
Prepare using PHILADELPHIA Neufchâtel Cheese.

**HOW TO SELECT SUGAR SNAP PEAS:**
Sugar snap peas are a cross between the common English pea and snow peas. Both the pod and peas inside are edible. Choose pods that are plump, crisp and bright green. Before using, snap off the stem ends, pulling to remove any strings.

# crust topped broccoli cheese bake

**PREP: 10 min. | TOTAL: 40 min. | MAKES: 14 servings.**

## ▸ what you need!

½ cup (½ of 8-oz. tub) PHILADELPHIA Chive & Onion Cream Cheese Spread

1 can (10¾ oz.) condensed cream of mushroom soup

½ cup water

2 pkg. (16 oz. each) frozen broccoli florets, thawed, drained

1 cup KRAFT Shredded Cheddar Cheese

1 thawed frozen puff pastry sheet (½ of 17.3-oz. pkg.)

1 egg, lightly beaten

## ▸ make it!

1. **HEAT** oven to 400°F.

2. **MIX** cream cheese spread, soup and water until well blended. Stir in broccoli and Cheddar. Spoon into 2½- to 3-qt. shallow rectangular or oval baking dish.

3. **ROLL** pastry sheet on lightly floured surface to fit baking dish. Cover dish completely with pastry. Press pastry edges against rim of dish to seal. Brush entire surface lightly with egg; pierce with knife five to six times to vent.

4. **BAKE** 30 min. or until heated through and pastry is puffed and golden brown.

**MAKE AHEAD:**
Assemble a day ahead; cover. Refrigerate overnight. When ready to serve, bake as directed.

**SUBSTITUTE:**
Prepare as directed, using PHILADELPHIA Chive & Onion Light Cream Cheese Spread and KRAFT 2% Milk Shredded Reduced Fat Cheddar Cheese.

# three-cheese chicken penne pasta bake

PREP: 20 min. | TOTAL: 43 min. | MAKES: 4 servings.

## ▸ what you need!

1½ cups multi-grain penne pasta, uncooked

1 pkg. (9 oz.) fresh spinach leaves

1 lb. boneless skinless chicken breasts, cut into bite-size pieces

1 tsp. dried basil leaves

1 jar (14½ oz.) spaghetti sauce

1 can (14½ oz.) diced tomatoes, drained

2 oz. (¼ of 8-oz. pkg.) PHILADELPHIA Neufchâtel Cheese, cubed

1 cup KRAFT 2% Milk Shredded Mozzarella Cheese, divided

2 Tbsp. KRAFT Grated Parmesan Cheese

## ▸ make it!

1. **HEAT** oven to 375°F.

2. **COOK** pasta as directed on package, adding spinach to the boiling water the last min.

3. **COOK** and stir chicken and basil in large nonstick skillet sprayed with cooking spray on medium-high heat 3 min. Stir in spaghetti sauce and tomatoes; bring to boil. Simmer on low heat 3 min. or until chicken is done. Stir in Neufchâtel.

4. **DRAIN** pasta mixture; return to pan. Stir in chicken mixture and ½ cup mozzarella. Spoon into 2-qt. casserole or 8-inch square baking dish.

5. **BAKE** 20 min. Sprinkle with remaining cheeses. Bake 3 min.

**SERVING SUGGESTION:**
Serve with CRYSTAL LIGHT Iced Tea.

# easy-bake cheddar biscuits

**PREP: 10 min. | TOTAL: 22 min. | MAKES: 9 servings.**

## ▶ what you need!

1 cup flour

2 tsp. CALUMET Baking Powder

¼ tsp. cream of tartar

¼ tsp. sugar

¼ tsp. salt

¼ cup cold butter, cut up

1 cup KRAFT Shredded Cheddar Cheese

⅓ cup milk

½ cup (½ of 8-oz. tub) PHILADELPHIA Chive & Onion Cream Cheese Spread

## ▶ make it!

1. **HEAT** oven to 450°F.

2. **MIX** first 5 ingredients in medium bowl. Cut in butter with pastry blender or two knives until mixture resembles coarse crumbs. Stir in Cheddar. Add milk; stir until mixture forms soft dough.

3. **PLACE** on lightly floured surface; knead 8 to 10 times or until smooth. Pat out dough into 6-inch square. Cut into 9 squares; place, 2 inches apart, on baking sheet.

4. **BAKE** 10 to 12 min. or until golden brown. Serve warm with cream cheese spread.

**SIZE-WISE:**
Enjoy your favorite foods on occasion, but remember to keep tabs on portions.

**FOR EASIER REMOVAL OF BISCUITS FROM BAKING SHEET:**
Baking sheet can be greased or covered with parchment paper before use for easier removal of biscuits.

# easy shepherd's pie

PREP: 10 min. | TOTAL: 30 min. | MAKES: 6 servings.

## ▶ what you need!

1 lb. ground beef

2 cups hot mashed potatoes

4 oz. (½ of 8-oz. pkg.) PHILADELPHIA Cream Cheese, cubed

1 cup KRAFT Shredded Cheddar Cheese, divided

2 cloves garlic, minced

4 cups frozen mixed vegetables, thawed

1 cup beef gravy

## ▶ make it!

1. **HEAT** oven to 375°F.

2. **BROWN** meat in large skillet; drain.

3. **MIX** potatoes, cream cheese, ½ cup Cheddar and garlic until well blended.

4. **COMBINE** meat, vegetables and gravy; spoon into 9-inch square baking dish.

5. **COVER** with potato mixture and remaining Cheddar. Bake 20 min. or until heated through.

**BARBECUE SHEPHERD'S PIE:**
Prepare omitting the garlic and substituting ¾ cup KRAFT Original Barbecue Sauce mixed with ½ tsp. onion powder for the gravy.

**CREATIVE LEFTOVERS:**
This recipe is a great way to use leftover mashed potatoes.

# ham & cheese pot pie

PREP: 15 min. | TOTAL: 47 min. | MAKES: 4 servings.

## ▶ what you need!

1 ham steak (6 oz.), chopped

1 cup KRAFT 2% Milk Shredded Cheddar Cheese

1 cup frozen broccoli cuts, thawed, drained

1 cup frozen cauliflower florets, thawed, drained

2 green onions, chopped

½ cup (½ of 8-oz. tub) PHILADELPHIA Chive & Onion ⅓ Less Fat than Cream Cheese

1 ready-to-use refrigerated pie crust (½ of 14.1-oz. pkg.)

1 egg

1 Tbsp. water

## ▶ make it!

1. **HEAT** oven to 400°F.

2. **COMBINE** first 5 ingredients. Microwave cream cheese spread in microwaveable bowl on HIGH 1 min. or until completely melted, stirring every 15 sec. Add to ham mixture; mix well. Spoon into 4 (6-oz.) ramekins.

3. **UNROLL** pie crust on lightly floured surface; roll to 12-inch circle. Cut into 4 circles with 5-inch round cookie cutter. Cut leaves from about ¼ of the trimmings with small cookie cutter or sharp knife; discard remaining trimmings.

4. **BEAT** egg and water until well blended; brush onto top edges of ramekins. Top with pie crust circles; press gently onto top edges of ramekins to seal. Top with leaf cutouts; brush lightly with egg wash. Discard any remaining egg wash. Place ramekins on baking sheet. Cut slits in crusts to vent.

5. **BAKE** 30 to 32 min. or until golden brown.

**NOTE:**
If you don't have a 5-inch cookie cutter, invert a 5-inch-diameter bowl or clean can onto pastry; trace around edge with small sharp knife. Repeat to cut out the remaining 3 circles.

**SUBSTITUTE:**
Prepare using KRAFT 2% Milk Shredded Colby & Monterey Jack Cheeses.

# potato-topped mini meatloaves

## ▶ what you need!

- 1 lb. ground beef
- 1 pkg. (6 oz.) STOVE TOP Stuffing Mix
- 1 cup water
- 2 Tbsp. A.1. Original Steak Sauce
- 6 oz. (¾ of 8-oz. pkg.) PHILADELPHIA Cream Cheese, cubed
- 3 cloves garlic, minced
- 3 cups hot mashed potatoes
- ¼ cup chopped fresh parsley
- 1 jar (12 oz.) beef gravy, warmed

## ▶ make it!

1. **HEAT** oven to 375°F.
2. **MIX** meat, stuffing mix, water and steak sauce; press into 12 muffin cups sprayed with cooking spray.
3. **BAKE** 20 to 25 min. or until done (160°F).
4. **ADD** cream cheese and garlic to potatoes; stir until cream cheese is melted. Stir in parsley. Scoop over meatloaves. Serve with gravy.

**SERVING SUGGESTION:**
Serve with a mixed green salad and glass of fat-free milk to round out the meal.

# spaghetti with zesty bolognese

**PREP: 10 min. | TOTAL: 30 min. | MAKES: 6 servings.**

## ▶ what you need!

1 small onion, chopped

¼ cup KRAFT Light Zesty Italian Dressing

1 lb. extra lean ground beef

1 can (15 oz.) tomato sauce

1 can (14 oz.) diced tomatoes, undrained

2 Tbsp. PHILADELPHIA Neufchâtel Cheese

12 oz. spaghetti, uncooked

¼ cup KRAFT Grated Parmesan Cheese

## ▶ make it!

1. **COOK** onions in dressing in large skillet on medium heat. Increase heat to medium-high. Add meat; cook, stirring frequently, until browned. Stir in tomato sauce and tomatoes. Bring to boil. Reduce heat to medium-low; simmer 15 min. Remove from heat. Stir in Neufchâtel until well blended.

2. **MEANWHILE,** cook pasta as directed on package.

3. **SPOON** sauce over pasta. Sprinkle with Parmesan.

**SUBSTITUTE:**
Prepare as directed using whole wheat or multi-grain spaghetti.

# easy cauliflower &
# broccoli au gratin

**PREP: 10 min. | TOTAL: 23 min. | MAKES: 10 servings, about ¾ cup each.**

## ▶ what you need!

5 cups broccoli florets

4 cups cauliflower florets

½ cup water

4 oz. (½ of 8-oz. pkg.) PHILADELPHIA Cream Cheese, cubed

¼ cup mllk

½ cup BREAKSTONE'S or KNUDSEN Sour Cream

1½ cups KRAFT Shredded Sharp Cheddar Cheese

10 RITZ Crackers, crushed

3 Tbsp. KRAFT Grated Parmesan Cheese

## ▶ make it!

1. **COMBINE** vegetables in 2-qt. microwaveable casserole. Add water; cover with lid. Microwave on HIGH 8 to 10 min. or until vegetables are tender; drain.

2. **MICROWAVE** cream cheese and milk in 2-cup microwaveable measuring cup 1 min. or until cream cheese is melted and mixture is well blended when stirred. Stir in sour cream; pour over vegetables. Sprinkle with Cheddar; microwave 2 min. or until melted.

3. **MIX** cracker crumbs and Parmesan; sprinkle over vegetables.

# zesty chicken pot pie

**PREP: 20 min. | TOTAL: 45 min. | MAKES: 8 servings.**

## ▶ what you need!

12 oz. (1½ pkg. [8 oz. each]) PHILADELPHIA Cream Cheese, cubed

½ cup chicken broth

3 cups chopped cooked chicken

2 pkg. (10 oz. each) frozen mixed vegetables, thawed

1 env. GOOD SEASONS Italian Salad Dressing & Recipe Mix

1 ready-to-use refrigerated pie crust (½ of 15-oz. pkg.)

## ▶ make it!

1. **HEAT** oven to 425°F.

2. **PLACE** cream cheese in large saucepan. Add broth; cook on low heat until cream cheese is completely melted, stirring frequently with wire whisk. Stir in chicken, vegetables and salad dressing mix.

3. **SPOON** into 9-inch pie plate. Cover with pie crust; seal and flute edge. Cut several slits in crust to allow steam to escape. Place pie plate on baking sheet.

4. **BAKE** 20 to 25 min. or until golden brown.

**SERVING SUGGESTION:**
Serve with a mixed green salad and glass of fat-free milk.

**MAKE AHEAD:**
Prepare as directed except for baking. Wrap securely; freeze. When ready to bake, unwrap. Place strips of foil around edge to prevent over browning. Bake frozen pie at 425°F for 1 hour and 10 min. or until heated through.

**SUBSTITUTES:**
Prepare as directed, using PHILADELPHIA Neufchâtel Cheese, GOOD SEASONS Zesty Italian Dressing or substituting turkey for the chicken.

# seafood enchiladas

PREP: 20 min. | TOTAL: 30 min. | MAKES: 10 servings, 1 enchilada each.

## ▶ what you need!

½ lb. cleaned shrimp, chopped

1 can (6 oz.) crabmeat, drained, flaked

1 can (7 oz.) whole kernel corn, drained

½ cup chopped green onions (about 2)

½ tsp. ground red pepper (cayenne), divided

1 pkg. (8 oz.) KRAFT 2% Milk Shredded Cheddar Cheese, divided

10 flour tortillas (7 inch)

4 oz. (½ of 8-oz. pkg.) PHILADELPHIA Cream Cheese, cubed

¾ cup milk

## ▶ make it!

1. **HEAT** oven to 350°F.

2. **COOK** and stir shrimp in medium nonstick skillet sprayed with cooking spray on medium heat 2 min. Add crabmeat, corn, onions and ¼ tsp. of the pepper; mix well. Cook and stir an additional 2 min. or until shrimp turn pink. Remove from heat. Stir in 1 cup Cheddar.

3. **SPOON** ⅓ cup of the seafood mixture onto each tortilla; roll up. Place, seam-sides down, in lightly greased 13×9-inch baking dish. Place cream cheese in medium saucepan. Add milk; cook on medium-low heat 5 min. or until cream cheese is completely melted and mixture is well blended, stirring frequently. Pour evenly over enchiladas.

4. **BAKE** 5 min. Remove from oven. Sprinkle with remaining Cheddar. Bake an additional 5 min. or until cheese is melted. Sprinkle with remaining ¼ tsp. pepper.

# Cheesecakes

A collection of our highest rated showstoppers

# silky chocolate cheesecake

PREP: 15 min. | TOTAL: 5 hours 10 min. | MAKES: 12 servings.

## ▶ what you need!

21  OREO Cookies, finely crushed (about 2 cups)

 2  Tbsp. sugar

⅓  cup butter or margarine, melted

 2  pkg. (4 oz. each) BAKER'S GERMAN'S Sweet Chocolate, divided

 2  eggs

⅔  cup corn syrup

⅓  cup whipping cream

1½  tsp. vanilla

 2  pkg. (8 oz. each) PHILADELPHIA Cream Cheese, cubed, softened

## ▶ make it!

1. **HEAT** oven to 325°F if using a silver 9-inch springform pan (or to 300°F if using a dark nonstick 9-inch springform pan).

2. **MIX** cookie crumbs, sugar and butter until well blended. Press firmly onto bottom and 1½ inches up sides of pan. Microwave 1½ packages (6 squares) of the chocolate in microwaveable bowl on HIGH 2 min., stirring after 1 min. Stir until chocolate is completely melted.

3. **PLACE** eggs, corn syrup, whipping cream and vanilla in blender container; cover. Blend until smooth. With blender running, gradually add cream cheese through small opening at top of blender, blending until smooth. Add melted chocolate; cover. Blend well. Pour into crust.

4. **BAKE** 50 to 55 min. or until center is almost set. Run knife or metal spatula around rim of pan to loosen cake; cool before removing from pan. Refrigerate 4 hours or overnight.

5. **MELT** remaining 2 squares of chocolate as directed on package. Drizzle over cheesecake just before serving. Store leftover cheesecake in refrigerator.

# cappuccino cheesecake

PREP: 25 min. | TOTAL: 6 hours 5 min. | MAKES: 16 servings.

## ▶ what you need!

- 1½ cups finely chopped PLANTERS Walnuts
- 3 Tbsp. butter or margarine, melted
- 2 Tbsp. sugar
- 4 pkg. (8 oz. each) PHILADELPHIA Cream Cheese, softened
- 1 cup sugar
- 3 Tbsp. flour
- 4 eggs
- 1 cup BREAKSTONE'S or KNUDSEN Sour Cream
- 1 Tbsp. MAXWELL HOUSE Instant Coffee
- ¼ tsp. ground cinnamon
- ¼ cup boiling water
- 1½ cups thawed COOL WHIP Whipped Topping

## ▶ make it!

1. **HEAT** oven to 325°F.

2. **MIX** nuts, butter and 2 Tbsp. sugar; press onto bottom of 9-inch springform pan. Bake 10 min. Remove from oven; cool. Increase oven temperature to 450°F.

3. **BEAT** cream cheese, 1 cup sugar and flour with mixer until well blended. Add eggs, 1 at a time, mixing on low speed after each just until blended. Blend in sour cream.

4. **DISSOLVE** instant coffee with cinnamon in water; cool. Gradually add to cream cheese mixture, mixing until well blended. Pour over crust.

5. **BAKE** 10 min. Reduce oven temperature to 250°F. Bake an additional 1 hour or until center is almost set. Run knife around rim of pan to loosen cake; cool before removing rim. Refrigerate 4 hours. Top with dollops of COOL WHIP. Garnish with a sprinkle of additional cinnamon, if desired.

**NOTE:**
Reduce oven temperature to 300°F if using a dark nonstick 9-inch springform pan.

# CHIPS AHOY!
# ice cream cheesecake

**PREP: 15 min. | TOTAL: 4 hours 15 min. | MAKES: 16 servings.**

## ▶ what you need!

1 pkg. (15.2 oz.) CHIPS AHOY! Cookies, divided

2 Tbsp. butter, melted

2 pkg. (8 oz. each) PHILADELPHIA Cream Cheese, softened

½ cup sugar

2 tsp. vanilla

1½ qt. (6 cups) vanilla ice cream, slightly softened

## ▶ make it!

1. **CRUSH** 20 cookies to form fine crumbs; mix with butter until well blended. Press onto bottom of 9-inch springform pan. Chop 16 of the remaining cookies.

2. **BEAT** cream cheese, sugar and vanilla in large bowl with mixer until well blended. Add ice cream; mix well. Stir in chopped cookies; pour over crust.

3. **FREEZE** 4 hours or until firm. Remove from freezer 10 min. before serving; let stand at room temperature to soften slightly. Top with remaining cookies.

# PHILADELPHIA 3-STEP white chocolate cheesecake

PREP: 10 min. | TOTAL: 3 hours 45 min. | MAKES: 8 servings.

## ▶ what you need!

- 2 pkg. (8 oz. each) PHILADELPHIA Cream Cheese, softened
- ½ cup sugar
- ½ tsp. vanilla
- 2 eggs
- 4 squares BAKER'S White Chocolate, chopped, divided
- 1 OREO Pie Crust (6 oz.)
- 16 candy-coated almonds

## ▶ make it!

**HEAT** oven to 350°F.

1. **BEAT** cream cheese, sugar and vanilla in large bowl with electric mixer on medium speed until well blended. Add eggs; mix just until blended. Stir in half of the white chocolate.

2. **POUR** into crust. Sprinkle with remaining white chocolate.

3. **BAKE** 35 min. or until center is almost set. Cool. Refrigerate 3 hours or overnight. Top with almonds just before serving. Store leftover cheesecake in refrigerator.

# chocolate-hazelnut cheesecake

**PREP: 30 min. | TOTAL: 5 hours 35 min. | MAKES: 16 servings.**

## ▶ what you need!

18 OREO Cookies, finely crushed (about 1½ cups)

2 Tbsp. butter or margarine, melted

3 pkg. (8 oz. each) PHILADELPHIA Cream Cheese, softened

1 cup sugar

1 tsp. vanilla

1 pkg. (8 squares) BAKER'S Semi-Sweet Chocolate, melted, slightly cooled

¼ cup hazelnut-flavored liqueur

3 eggs

½ cup whole hazelnuts, toasted

## ▶ make it!

1. **HEAT** oven to 325°F if using a silver 9-inch springform pan (or to 300°F if using a dark nonstick 9-inch springform pan).

2. **MIX** crushed cookies and butter; press firmly onto bottom of pan. Bake 10 min.

3. **BEAT** cream cheese, sugar and vanilla in large bowl with electric mixer on medium speed until well blended. Add chocolate and liqueur; mix well. Add eggs, 1 at a time, mixing on low speed after each addition just until blended. Pour over crust.

4. **BAKE** 55 min. to 1 hour 5 min. or until center is almost set. Run knife or metal spatula around rim of pan to loosen cake; cool before removing rim of pan. Refrigerate 4 hours or overnight. Top with nuts just before serving.

# frozen lemon cheesecake with blueberry drizzle

PREP: 20 min. | TOTAL: 6 hours 20 min. | MAKES: 16 servings.

## ▶ what you need!

24  NABISCO Ginger Snaps, crushed (about 1½ cups)

¼  cup butter, melted

2  pkg. (8 oz. each) PHILADELPHIA Cream Cheese, softened

1  can (14 oz.) sweetened condensed milk

1  Tbsp. lemon zest

¼  cup lemon juice

1  cup thawed COOL WHIP Whipped Topping

2  cups blueberries

¼  cup sugar

2  Tbsp. water

¼  tsp. ground ginger

## ▶ make it!

1. **MIX** cookie crumbs and butter; press onto bottom of 9-inch springform pan.

2. **BEAT** cream cheese in large bowl with mixer until creamy. Gradually beat in sweetened condensed milk. Blend in lemon zest and juice. Whisk in COOL WHIP; spoon over crust.

3. **FREEZE** 6 hours or until firm. Meanwhile, cook remaining ingredients in saucepan on medium heat 4 min. stirring occasionally; cool. Refrigerate until ready to serve.

4. **REMOVE** cheesecake from freezer 15 min. before serving. Let stand at room temperature to soften slightly. Serve topped with blueberry sauce.

**SIZE-WISE:**
Since this indulgent cheesecake makes 16 servings, it's the perfect dessert to serve at your next party!

**HOW TO CRUSH GINGER SNAPS:**
Place ginger snaps in food processor; process until finely crushed.

# german chocolate cheesecake

**PREP: 30 min. | TOTAL: 4 hours 20 min. | MAKES: 14 servings.**

## ▶ what you need!

1 cup finely crushed FAMOUS Chocolate Wafers

1 cup sugar, divided

3 Tbsp. butter or margarine, melted

3 pkg. (8 oz. each) PHILADELPHIA Cream Cheese, softened

¼ cup flour

1 pkg. (4 oz.) BAKER'S GERMAN'S Sweet Chocolate, melted

2½ tsp. vanilla, divided

4 eggs, divided

⅓ cup canned evaporated milk

¼ cup butter or margarine

½ cup BAKER'S ANGEL FLAKE Coconut

½ cup PLANTERS Chopped Pecans

## ▶ make it!

1. **HEAT** oven to 350°F.

2. **MIX** crushed wafers, 2 Tbsp. of the sugar and 3 Tbsp. butter; press firmly onto bottom of 9-inch springform pan. Bake 10 min.

3. **BEAT** cream cheese, ½ cup of the sugar and the flour in large bowl with electric mixer on medium speed until well blended. Add chocolate and 2 tsp. of the vanilla; mix well. Add 3 of the eggs, 1 at a time, mixing on low speed after each addition just until blended. Pour over crust.

4. **BAKE** 45 to 50 min. or until center is almost set. Run knife or metal spatula around rim of pan to loosen cake; cool before removing rim of pan. Refrigerate 4 hours or overnight.

5. **PLACE** milk, remaining sugar, the ¼ cup butter, remaining egg and remaining ½ tsp. vanilla in small saucepan; cook on medium-low heat until thickened, stirring constantly. Stir in coconut and nuts. Cool. Spread over cheesecake just before serving. Store leftover cheesecake in refrigerator.

**SIZE-WISE:**
Since this indulgent special-occasion dessert makes 14 servings, it's a perfect dessert to serve at your next party.

**HOW TO MELT CHOCOLATE:**
Unwrap chocolate; break in half. Place in microwaveable bowl. Microwave on HIGH 1½ min., stirring after 1 min. Stir until chocolate is completely melted.

# marbled white chocolate cheesecake

PREP: 15 min. | TOTAL: 4 hours 55 min. | MAKES: 12 servings.

## ▶ what you need!

1½ cups crushed FAMOUS Chocolate Wafers

3 Tbsp. butter or margarine, melted

3 pkg. (8 oz. each) PHILADELPHIA Cream Cheese, softened

½ cup sugar

½ tsp. vanilla

3 eggs

2 squares BAKER'S Semi-Sweet Chocolate, melted

1 pkg. (6 squares) BAKER'S White Chocolate, melted

## ▶ make it!

1. **HEAT** oven to 350°F if using a silver 9-inch springform pan (or to 325°F if using a dark nonstick 9-inch springform pan).

2. **MIX** crushed wafers and butter. Press firmly onto bottom of pan. Bake 10 min.

3. **BEAT** cream cheese, sugar and vanilla in large bowl with electric mixer on medium speed until well blended. Add eggs, 1 at a time, mixing on low speed after each addition just until blended. Remove 1 cup of the cream cheese mixture; place in small bowl. Add melted semi-sweet chocolate; stir until well blended. Add melted white chocolate to remaining cream cheese mixture; mix well. Spoon semi-sweet and white chocolate mixtures alternately over crust. Swirl with knife to marbleize.

4. **BAKE** 40 min. or until center is almost set. Run small knife or spatula around side of pan to loosen cake; cool before removing rim of pan. Refrigerate 4 hours or overnight. Store leftover cheesecake in refrigerator.

# NILLA praline cheesecake

**PREP: 20 min. | TOTAL: 6 hours 5 min. | MAKES: 16 servings.**

## ▶ what you need!

66 NILLA Wafers, divided

1¼ cups sugar, divided

¼ cup margarine or butter, melted

3 pkg. (8 oz. each) PHILADELPHIA Cream Cheese, softened

½ cup BREAKSTONE'S or KNUDSEN Sour Cream

1 tsp. vanilla

3 eggs

25 KRAFT Caramels

3 Tbsp. milk

½ cup PLANTERS Pecan Pieces, toasted

## ▶ make it!

1. **HEAT** oven to 325°F.

2. **FINELY** crush 50 wafers; mix with ¼ cup sugar and margarine. Press onto bottom of 9-inch springform pan. Stand remaining wafers around edge, pressing gently into crust to secure.

3. **BEAT** cream cheese and remaining sugar in large bowl with mixer until well blended. Add sour cream and vanilla; mix well. Add eggs, 1 at a time, beating on low speed after each just until blended. Pour over crust.

4. **BAKE** 45 to 50 min. or until center is almost set. Run small knife around rim of pan to loosen cake; cool before removing rim. Refrigerate 4 hours. Microwave caramels and milk on HIGH 1 min. or until caramels are completely melted, stirring every 30 sec. Cool slightly. Pour over cheesecake; top with nuts.

**SUBSTITUTE:**
Line 13×9-inch pan with foil, with ends of foil extending over sides. Grease foil. Prepare recipe as directed, increasing whole NILLA Wafers around the side from 16 to 22. Bake 40 to 45 min. or until center is almost set. Use foil handles to lift dessert from pan before cutting into squares to serve.

**NOTE:**
If using a dark nonstick 9-inch springform pan, reduce oven temperature to 300°F.

**HOW TO TOAST NUTS:**
Toasting nuts adds crunch and intensifies their flavor. To toast nuts in the oven, spread nuts in single layer in shallow baking pan. Bake at 350°F for 10 to 15 min. or until golden brown, stirring occasionally.

# OREO cheesecake bites

**PREP: 20 min. | TOTAL: 5 hours 5 min. | MAKES: 36 servings, 1 bar each.**

## ▶ what you need!

36 OREO Cookies, divided

½ cup butter or margarine, divided

4 pkg. (8 oz. each) PHILADELPHIA Cream Cheese, softened

1 cup sugar

1 tsp. vanilla

1 cup BREAKSTONE'S or KNUDSEN Sour Cream

4 eggs

4 squares BAKER'S Semi-Sweet Chocolate

## ▶ make it!

1. **HEAT** oven to 325°F.

2. **LINE** 13×9-inch baking pan with foil. Finely crush 24 cookies. Melt ¼ cup butter; mix with crumbs. Press onto bottom of pan.

3. **BEAT** cream cheese, sugar and vanilla with mixer until blended. Add sour cream; mix well. Add eggs, 1 at a time, beating just until blended after each addition. Chop remaining cookies. Gently stir into batter; pour over crust.

4. **BAKE** 45 min. or until center is almost set. Cool. Meanwhile, place chocolate and remaining ¼ cup butter in microwaveable bowl. Microwave on HIGH 1 min. Stir until smooth. Cool slightly; pour over cheesecake. Spread to cover top of cheesecake. Refrigerate at least 4 hours. Remove cheesecake from pan before cutting to serve.

**HOW TO MAKE MESS-FREE COOKIE CRUMBS:**
Crushing cookies into crumbs can be a messy task. To keep the mess to a minimum, place the whole cookies in a resealable plastic bag. Flatten bag to remove excess air, then seal bag. Crush the cookies into crumbs by rolling a rolling pin across the bag until the crumbs are as fine as you need.

**HOW TO NEATLY CUT DESSERT BARS:**
When cutting creamy-textured bars, such as these cheesecake bites, carefully wipe off the knife blade between cuts with a clean damp towel. This prevents the creamy filling from building up on the blade, ensuring clean cuts that leave the edges intact.

**NOTE:**
When lining pan with foil, extend ends of foil over sides of pan to use as handles when removing cheesecake from pan.

# cranberry-cinnamon cheesecake

**PREP: 20 min. | TOTAL: 5 hours 40 min. | MAKES: 16 servings.**

## ▶ what you need!

1½ cups HONEY MAID Graham Cracker Crumbs

1½ cups sugar, divided

1 tsp. ground cinnamon, divided

¼ cup butter, melted

4 pkg. (8 oz. each) PHILADELPHIA Cream Cheese, softened

4 eggs

1½ cups fresh cranberries (½ of 12-oz. pkg.)

½ cup water

1½ cups thawed COOL WHIP Whipped Topping

## ▶ make it!

1. **HEAT** oven to 325°F.

2. **MIX** graham crumbs, 2 Tbsp. sugar, ½ tsp. cinnamon and butter until well blended; press onto bottom of 9-inch springform pan.

3. **BEAT** cream cheese and 1 cup of the remaining sugar in large bowl with mixer until well blended. Add eggs, 1 at a time, mixing on low speed after each just until blended. Pour over crust.

4. **BAKE** 55 min. to 1 hour 5 min. or until center is almost set. Cool on rack 15 min. Run knife around rim of pan to loosen cake; cool before removing rim. Refrigerate 4 hours.

5. **MEANWHILE,** bring cranberries, water and remaining sugar and cinnamon to boil in saucepan on medium-high heat; simmer on low heat 8 to 10 min. or until sauce is slightly thickened and berries have softened, stirring occasionally. Cool slightly; refrigerate until ready to serve.

6. **SPREAD** cranberry sauce over cheesecake just before serving. Serve with COOL WHIP.

# PHILADELPHIA 3-STEP
## strawberry layer cheesecake

**PREP: 10 min. | TOTAL: 3 hours 50 min. | MAKES: 8 servings.**

## ▶ what you need!

2 pkg. (8 oz. each) PHILADELPHIA Cream Cheese, softened

½ cup sugar

½ tsp. vanilla

2 eggs

¼ cup strawberry preserves

5 drops red food coloring

1 HONEY MAID Graham Pie Crust (6 oz.)

1 cup thawed COOL WHIP Whipped Topping

4 medium strawberries, sliced

## ▶ make it!

**HEAT** oven to 350°F.

1. **BEAT** cream cheese, sugar and vanilla with electric mixer on medium speed until well blended. Add eggs; mix just until blended. Remove 1 cup of the batter. Add preserves and food coloring; stir until well blended. Pour into crust; cover with the remaining plain batter.

2. **BAKE** 40 min. or until center is almost set. Cool.

3. **REFRIGERATE** 3 hours or overnight. Top with COOL WHIP and strawberries just before serving. Store leftover cheesecake in refrigerator.

**GREAT SUBSTITUTE:**
Prepare as directed, using a NILLA Pie Crust.

# PHILADELPHIA 3-STEP
# mini cheesecakes

**PREP: 10 min. | TOTAL: 3 hours 30 min. | MAKES: 12 servings.**

## ▶ what you need!

2 pkg. (8 oz. each) PHILADELPHIA Cream Cheese, softened

½ cup sugar

½ tsp. vanilla

2 eggs

12 OREO Cookies

1 kiwi, peeled, cut into 6 slices

36 blueberries (about ½ cup)

12 raspberries (about ⅓ cup)

## ▶ make it!

**HEAT** oven to 350°F.

1. **BEAT** cream cheese, sugar and vanilla in large bowl with electric mixer on medium speed until well blended. Add eggs, 1 at a time, beating on low speed after each addition just until blended.

2. **PLACE** 1 cookie in bottom of each of 12 medium paper-lined muffin cups. Fill evenly with batter.

3. **BAKE** 20 min. or until centers are almost set. Cool. Refrigerate 3 hours or overnight. Cut kiwi slices in half. Top each cheesecake with 1 kiwi half, 3 blueberries and 1 raspberry just before serving.

**VARIATION:**

**Cheesecake Squares:** Line 8-inch square baking pan with foil. Mix 1½ cups finely crushed OREO Cookies or HONEY MAID Honey Grahams with ¼ cup melted butter; press firmly onto bottom of pan. Prepare cheesecake batter as directed. Pour over crust. Bake and refrigerate as directed. Cut into 16 squares. Top evenly with the fruit mixture just before serving. Makes 16 servings, 1 square each.

# prize winning chocolate cheesecake

**PREP: 20 min. | TOTAL: 4 hours 20 min. | MAKES: 10 servings.**

## ▶ what you need!

1½ cups TEDDY GRAHAMS Chocolate Graham Snacks, crushed

¾ cup PLANTERS Sliced Almonds, finely chopped

¼ cup butter, melted

1 tsp. vanilla, divided

2 pkg. (8 oz. each) PHILADELPHIA Cream Cheese, softened

½ cup sugar

1 jar (13 oz.) chocolate-hazelnut spread

1 tub (8 oz.) COOL WHIP Whipped Topping, thawed

## ▶ make it!

1. **MIX** graham crumbs, nuts, butter and ½ tsp. vanilla until well blended; press onto bottom and up sides of 9-inch pie plate. Refrigerate until ready to use.

2. **BEAT** cream cheese and sugar in large bowl with mixer until well blended. Add hazelnut spread and remaining vanilla; mix well. Stir in COOL WHIP; spoon into crust.

3. **REFRIGERATE** 4 hours.

   **SUBSTITUTE:**
   Prepare using COOL WHIP Extra Creamy Whipped Topping.

# PHILADELPHIA 3-STEP
## coconut cheesecake

PREP: 10 min. | TOTAL: 4 hours 50 min. | MAKES: 10 servings.

## ▶ what you need!

2 pkg. (8 oz. each) PHILADELPHIA Cream Cheese, softened

½ cup cream of coconut

½ cup sugar

½ tsp. vanilla

2 eggs

1 HONEY MAID Graham Pie Crust (6 oz.)

2 cups thawed COOL WHIP Whipped Topping

½ cup BAKER'S ANGEL FLAKE Coconut, toasted

## ▶ make it!

**HEAT** oven to 350°F.

1. **BEAT** cream cheese, cream of coconut, sugar and vanilla with electric mixer on medium speed until well blended. Add eggs; mix just until blended.

2. **POUR** into crust.

3. **BAKE** 40 min. or until center is almost set. Cool. Refrigerate 3 hours or overnight. Top with COOL WHIP and toasted coconut just before serving. Store leftover cheesecake in refrigerator.

# PHILADELPHIA new york-style sour cream-topped cheesecake

PREP: 15 min. | TOTAL: 5 hours 5 min. | MAKES: 16 servings.

## ▶ what you need!

1½ cups HONEY MAID Graham Cracker Crumbs

¼ cup butter, melted

1¼ cups sugar, divided

4 pkg. (8 oz. each) PHILADELPHIA Cream Cheese, softened

2 tsp. vanilla, divided

1 container (16 oz.) BREAKSTONE'S or KNUDSEN Sour Cream, divided

4 eggs

2 cups fresh strawberries, sliced

## ▶ make it!

1. **HEAT** oven to 325°F.

2. **LINE** 13×9-inch pan with foil, with ends of foil extending over sides of pan. Mix graham crumbs, butter and 2 Tbsp. sugar; press onto bottom of pan.

3. **BEAT** cream cheese, 1 cup of remaining sugar and 1 tsp. vanilla in large bowl with mixer until well blended. Add 1 cup sour cream; mix well. Add eggs, 1 at a time, beating on low speed after each just until blended. Pour over crust.

4. **BAKE** 40 min. or until center is almost set. Mix remaining sour cream, sugar and vanilla; carefully spread over cheesecake. Bake 10 min. Cool completely. Refrigerate 4 hours. Use foil handles to lift cheesecake from pan just before serving; top with berries.

**SUBSTITUTE:**
Substitute 1½ cups finely crushed OREO Cookies for the graham cracker crumbs.

# PHILADELPHIA new york-style strawberry swirl cheesecake

**PREP: 15 min. | TOTAL: 5 hours 25 min. | MAKES: 16 servings.**

## ▶ what you need!

1 cup HONEY MAID Graham Cracker Crumbs

3 Tbsp. sugar

3 Tbsp. butter, melted

5 pkg. (8 oz. each) PHILADELPHIA Cream Cheese, softened

1 cup sugar

3 Tbsp. flour

1 Tbsp. vanilla

1 cup BREAKSTONE'S or KNUDSEN Sour Cream

4 eggs

⅓ cup seedless strawberry jam

## ▶ make it!

1. **HEAT** oven to 325°F.

2. **LINE** 13×9-inch pan with foil, with ends of foil extending over sides. Mix graham crumbs, 3 Tbsp. sugar and butter; press onto bottom of pan. Bake 10 min.

3. **BEAT** cream cheese, 1 cup sugar, flour and vanilla in large bowl with mixer until well blended. Add sour cream; mix well. Add eggs, 1 at a time, mixing on low speed after each just until blended. Pour over crust. Gently drop small spoonfuls of jam over batter; swirl with knife.

4. **BAKE** 40 min. or until center is almost set. Cool completely. Refrigerate 4 hours. Lift cheesecake from pan with foil handles before cutting to serve.

# PHILADELPHIA triple-chocolate cheesecake

**PREP: 20 min. | TOTAL: 5 hours 45 min. | MAKES: 16 servings.**

## ▶ what you need!

24 OREO Cookies, finely crushed (about 2 cups)

2 Tbsp. butter or margarine, melted

1 pkg. (6 squares) BAKER'S White Chocolate, divided

4 pkg. (8 oz. each) PHILADELPHIA Cream Cheese, softened, divided

1 cup sugar, divided

½ tsp. vanilla

3 eggs

3 squares BAKER'S Semi-Sweet Chocolate, divided

1 tub (8 oz.) COOL WHIP Whipped Topping, thawed

## ▶ make it!

1. **HEAT** oven to 325°F.

2. **MIX** cookie crumbs and butter; press onto bottom of 9-inch springform pan. Melt 5 white chocolate squares as directed on package; cool slightly.

3. **BEAT** 3 packages cream cheese, ¾ cup sugar and vanilla with mixer until well blended. Add melted white chocolate; mix well. Add eggs, 1 at a time, mixing on low speed after each just until blended. Pour over crust.

4. **BAKE** 50 to 55 min. or until center is almost set. Run knife around rim of pan to loosen cake; cool completely. Meanwhile, melt 2 semi-sweet chocolate squares; cool.

5. **BEAT** remaining cream cheese and sugar in large bowl until well blended. Add melted semi-sweet chocolate; mix well. Whisk in COOL WHIP; spread over cheesecake. Refrigerate 4 hours. Garnish with chocolate curls from remaining white and semi-sweet chocolates.

**SIZE WISE:**
Need a sweet treat to serve a crowd? Try this chocolatey dessert! Since it serves 16 people, it easily fits the bill.

**VARIATION:**
Substitute foil-lined 13×9-inch pan for the springform pan. Mix crust ingredients as directed. Press onto bottom of prepared pan; cover with prepared filling. Bake 45 min. or until center is almost set. Cool completely in pan. Spread with COOL WHIP mixture. Refrigerate 4 hours. Use ends of foil to remove cheesecake from pan before cutting to serve.

**HOW TO SHAVE CHOCOLATE:**
Warm 1 chocolate square by microwaving it on HIGH for a few sec. or just until you can smudge the chocolate with your thumb. Hold square steadily, then draw a vegetable peeler slowly over the chocolate to form shavings. Repeat with remaining chocolate square.

# PHILADELPHIA vanilla mousse cheesecake

**PREP: 20 min. | TOTAL: 6 hours 15 min. | MAKES: 16 servings.**

## ▶ what you need!

40 NILLA Wafers, crushed (about 1½ cups)

3 Tbsp. butter or margarine, melted

4 pkg. (8 oz. each) PHILADELPHIA Cream Cheese, softened, divided

1 cup sugar, divided

1 Tbsp. plus 1 tsp. vanilla, divided

3 eggs

1 tub (8 oz.) COOL WHIP Whipped Topping, thawed

## ▶ make it!

1. **HEAT** oven to 325°F.

2. **MIX** wafer crumbs and butter; press onto bottom of 9-inch springform pan.

3. **BEAT** 3 packages cream cheese, ¾ cup sugar and 1 Tbsp. vanilla with mixer until well blended. Add eggs, 1 at a time, mixing on low speed after each just until blended. Pour over crust.

4. **BAKE** 50 to 55 min. or until center is almost set. Run knife around rim of pan to loosen cake; cool completely in pan.

5. **BEAT** remaining cream cheese, sugar and vanilla with mixer in large bowl until well blended. Whisk in COOL WHIP; spread over cheesecake. Refrigerate 4 hours. Remove rim of pan before serving cheesecake.

**SIZE-WISE:**
Need a sweet treat to serve a crowd? Try this rich, creamy dessert! Since it serves 16 people, it easily fits the bill.

**VANILLA BEAN MOUSSE CHEESECAKE:**
Prepare recipe as directed, using a vanilla bean and reducing vanilla extract to 2 tsp. Use sharp knife to gently split 1 vanilla bean pod lengthwise in half, then scrape seeds into cheesecake batter. Add 1 tsp. vanilla extract to the batter and use remaining extract to flavor cheesecake topping as directed.

**SPECIAL EXTRA:**
Garnish with fresh berries just before serving.

# PHILADELPHIA white chocolate-peppermint cheesecake

**PREP: 15 min. | TOTAL: 5 hours 35 min. | MAKES: 16 servings.**

## ▸ what you need!

1½ cups HONEY MAID Graham Cracker Crumbs

3 Tbsp. sugar

¼ cup butter, melted

4 pkg. (8 oz. each) PHILADELPHIA Cream Cheese, softened

1 cup sugar

¼ tsp. peppermint extract

1 cup BREAKSTONE'S or KNUDSEN Sour Cream

4 squares BAKER'S White Chocolate, melted

4 eggs

1 cup thawed COOL WHIP Whipped Topping

16 starlight mints

## ▸ make it!

1. **HEAT** oven to 325°F.

2. **LINE** 13×9-inch pan with foil, with ends of foil extending over sides of pan. Mix graham crumbs, 3 Tbsp. sugar and butter; press onto bottom of pan. Bake 10 min.

3. **BEAT** cream cheese, 1 cup sugar and extract in large bowl with mixer until well blended. Add sour cream and chocolate; mix well. Add eggs, 1 at a time, mixing on low speed after each just until blended. Pour over crust.

4. **BAKE** 40 min. or until center is almost set. Cool. Refrigerate 4 hours. Use foil handles to lift cheesecake from pan before cutting to serve. Top each piece with a dollop of COOL WHIP and a mint just before serving.

**SERVING SUGGESTION:**
This is a great dessert to share at a holiday party. At 16 servings, there's enough for a crowd.

# PHILLY blueberry swirl cheesecake

**PREP: 15 min. | TOTAL: 5 hours | MAKES: 16 servings.**

## ▸ what you need!

    1 cup HONEY MAID Graham Cracker Crumbs

    1 cup plus 3 Tbsp. sugar, divided

    3 Tbsp. butter or margarine, melted

    4 pkg. (8 oz. each) PHILADELPHIA Cream Cheese, softened

    1 tsp. vanilla

    1 cup BREAKSTONE'S or KNUDSEN Sour Cream

    4 eggs

    2 cups fresh or thawed frozen blueberries

## ▸ make it!

1. **HEAT** oven to 325°F.

2. **MIX** graham crumbs, 3 Tbsp. of the sugar and butter. Press firmly onto bottom of foil-lined 13×9-inch baking pan. Bake 10 min.

3. **BEAT** cream cheese, remaining 1 cup sugar and vanilla in large bowl with electric mixer on medium speed until well blended. Add sour cream; mix well. Add eggs, 1 at a time, beating on low speed after each addition just until blended. Pour over crust. Purée blueberries in a blender or food processor. Gently drop spoonfuls of puréed blueberries over batter; cut through batter several times with knife for marble effect.

4. **BAKE** 45 min. or until center is almost set; cool. Cover and refrigerate at least 4 hours before serving. Garnish as desired. Store leftover cheesecake in refrigerator.

**SUBSTITUTE:**
Substitute 1 can (15 oz.) blueberries, well drained, for the 2 cups fresh or frozen blueberries.

**MAKE IT EASY:**
Instead of using a blender, crush the blueberries in a bowl with a fork. Drain before spooning over the cheesecake batter and swirling to marbleize as directed.

# PHILADELPHIA
# classic cheesecake

**PREP: 20 min. | TOTAL: 5 hours 45 min. | MAKES: 16 servings.**

## ▶ what you need!

1½ cups HONEY MAID Graham Cracker Crumbs

3 Tbsp. sugar

⅓ cup butter or margarine, melted

4 pkg. (8 oz. each) PHILADELPHIA Cream Cheese, softened

1 cup sugar

1 tsp. vanilla

4 eggs

## ▶ make it!

1. **HEAT** oven to 325°F.

2. **MIX** graham crumbs, 3 Tbsp. sugar and butter; press onto bottom of 9-inch springform pan.

3. **BEAT** cream cheese, 1 cup sugar and vanilla with mixer until well blended. Add eggs, 1 at a time, mixing on low speed after each just until blended. Pour over crust.

4. **BAKE** 55 min. or until center is almost set. Loosen cake from rim of pan; cool before removing rim. Refrigerate 4 hours.

# chocolate turtle cheesecake

**PREP: 15 min. | TOTAL: 5 hours 50 min. | MAKES: 16 servings.**

## ▶ what you need!

1½ cups crushed NILLA Wafers (about 50)

¾ cup chopped PLANTERS Pecans, divided

¼ cup butter, melted

32 KRAFT Caramels

3 Tbsp. milk

4 pkg. (8 oz. each) PHILADELPHIA Cream Cheese, softened

1 cup sugar

1 cup BREAKSTONE'S or KNUDSEN Sour Cream

4 eggs

1 pkg. (8 squares) BAKER'S Semi-Sweet Chocolate, divided

## ▶ make it!

1. **HEAT** oven to 325°F.

2. **MIX** wafer crumbs, ½ cup nuts and butter; press onto bottom of 13×9-inch pan. Microwave caramels and milk in microwaveable bowl on MEDIUM (50%) 4 to 5 min. or until caramels are melted and mixture is well blended, stirring every 2 min. Pour over crust; spread to within 1 inch of edge. Cool.

3. **BEAT** cream cheese and sugar with mixer until blended. Add sour cream; mix well. Add eggs, 1 at a time, mixing on low speed after each just until blended. Melt 7 chocolate squares. Stir into cream cheese batter; pour over caramel layer.

4. **BAKE** 45 to 50 min. or until center is almost set. Cool completely. Refrigerate 4 hours. Sprinkle with remaining nuts just before serving. Melt remaining chocolate square; drizzle over cheesecake.

# pumpkin swirl cheesecake

PREP: 20 min. | TOTAL: 5 hours 35 min. | MAKES: 16 servings.

## ▶ what you need!

25 NABISCO Ginger Snaps, finely crushed (about 1½ cups)

½ cup finely chopped PLANTERS Pecans

¼ cup butter, melted

4 pkg. (8 oz. each) PHILADELPHIA Cream Cheese, softened

1 cup sugar, divided

1 tsp. vanilla

4 eggs

1 cup canned pumpkin

1 tsp. ground cinnamon

¼ tsp. ground nutmeg

Dash ground cloves

## ▶ make it!

1. **HEAT** oven to 325°F.

2. **LINE** 13×9-inch pan with foil, with ends of foil extending over sides. Mix cookie crumbs, nuts and butter; press onto bottom of pan.

3. **BEAT** cream cheese, ¾ cup sugar and vanilla with mixer until well blended. Add eggs, 1 at a time, mixing on low speed after each just until blended. Remove 1½ cups batter; place in small bowl. Stir remaining sugar, pumpkin and spices into remaining batter. Spoon half the pumpkin batter over crust; top with spoonfuls of half the plain batter. Repeat layers; swirl gently with knife.

4. **BAKE** 45 min. or until center is almost set. Cool completely. Refrigerate 4 hours. Use foil handles to lift cheesecake from pan before cutting to serve.

**SIZE-WISE:**
Sweets can add enjoyment to a balanced diet, but remember to keep tabs on portions.

# ribbon bar cheesecake

PREP: 15 min. | TOTAL: 5 hours 15 min. | MAKES: 16 servings, 1 square each.

## ▶ what you need!

30  OREO Cookies, crushed

½  cup butter, melted

¼  cup chopped PLANTERS Pecans

¼  cup BAKER'S ANGEL FLAKE Coconut

4  pkg. (8 oz. each) PHILADELPHIA Cream Cheese, softened

1  cup sugar

4  eggs

½  cup whipping cream

6  squares BAKER'S Semi-Sweet Chocolate

## ▶ make it!

1. **HEAT** oven to 350°F.

2. **MIX** crushed cookies, butter, nuts and coconut; press firmly onto bottom of 13×9-inch baking pan. Refrigerate while preparing filling.

3. **BEAT** cream cheese and sugar in large bowl with electric mixer on medium speed until well blended. Add eggs, 1 at a time, mixing on low speed after each addition just until blended. Pour over crust.

4. **BAKE** 40 min. or until center is almost set. Cool. Refrigerate 3 hours or overnight. Place whipping cream and chocolate in saucepan. Cook on low heat until chocolate is completely melted and mixture is well blended, stirring occasionally. Pour over cheesecake. Refrigerate 15 min. or until chocolate is firm. Store leftover cheesecake in refrigerator.

**JAZZ IT UP:**
After chocolate topping is firm, place 1 additional chocolate square in microwaveable bowl. Microwave on MEDIUM 1 min., stirring after 30 sec. Stir until chocolate is completely melted. Pour into small resealable bag; seal bag. Snip off one small corner from bottom of bag; twist top of bag to squeeze chocolate from bag to pipe a special message, such as "Greetings," on top of cheesecake.

# triple-citrus cheesecake

**PREP: 30 min. | TOTAL: 6 hours 35 min. | MAKES: 16 servings.**

## ▶ what you need!

1 cup HONEY MAID Graham Cracker Crumbs

⅓ cup firmly packed brown sugar

¼ cup butter or margarine, melted

4 pkg. (8 oz. each) PHILADELPHIA Cream Cheese, softened

1 cup granulated sugar

2 Tbsp. flour

1 tsp. vanilla

4 eggs

1 Tbsp. fresh lemon juice

1 Tbsp. fresh lime juice

1 Tbsp. fresh orange juice

1 Tbsp. grated lemon zest

1 Tbsp. grated lime zest

1 Tbsp. grated orange zest

## ▶ make it!

1. **HEAT** oven to 325°F if using a silver 9-inch springform pan (or to 300°F if using a dark nonstick 9-inch springform pan).

2. **MIX** graham crumbs, brown sugar and butter; press firmly onto bottom of pan. Bake 10 min.

3. **BEAT** cream cheese, granulated sugar, flour and vanilla with electric mixer on medium speed until well blended. Add eggs, 1 at a time, mixing on low speed after each addition just until blended. Stir in remaining ingredients; pour over crust.

4. **BAKE** 1 hour and 5 min. or until center is almost set. Run knife or metal spatula around rim of pan to loosen cake; cool before removing rim of pan. Refrigerate 4 hours or overnight. Store leftover cheesecake in refrigerator.

# ultimate turtle cheesecake

**PREP: 30 min. | TOTAL: 6 hours 10 min. | MAKES: 16 servings.**

## ▶ what you need!

24 OREO Cookies, finely crushed

6 Tbsp. butter or margarine, melted

1 pkg. (14 oz.) KRAFT Caramels

½ cup milk

1 cup chopped PLANTERS Pecans

3 pkg. (8 oz. each) PHILADELPHIA Cream Cheese, softened

¾ cup sugar

1 Tbsp. vanilla

3 eggs

2 squares BAKER'S Semi-Sweet Chocolate

## ▶ make it!

1. **HEAT** oven to 325°F.

2. **MIX** cookie crumbs and butter; press onto bottom and 2 inches up sides of 9-inch springform pan.

3. **MICROWAVE** caramels and milk in small microwaveable bowl on HIGH 3 min. or until caramels are completely melted, stirring after each minute. Stir in nuts; pour half into crust. Refrigerate 10 min. Refrigerate remaining caramel mixture for later use.

4. **BEAT** cream cheese, sugar and vanilla with mixer until well blended. Add eggs, 1 at a time, mixing on low speed after each just until blended. Pour over caramel layer in crust.

5. **BAKE** 1 hour 5 min. to 1 hour 10 min. or until center is almost set. Run knife around rim of pan to loosen cake; cool before removing rim. Refrigerate 4 hours.

6. **MICROWAVE** reserved caramel mixture 1 min.; stir. Pour over cheesecake. Melt chocolate as directed on package; drizzle over cheesecake.

# white chocolate-cherry pecan cheesecake

**PREP: 30 min.** | **TOTAL: 6 hours 30 min.** | **MAKES: 16 servings.**

## ▶ what you need!

- 1 cup PLANTERS Pecan Halves, toasted, divided
- 1½ cups HONEY MAID Graham Cracker Crumbs
- ¼ cup sugar
- ¼ cup margarine or butter, melted
- 3 pkg. (8 oz. each) PHILADELPHIA Cream Cheese, softened
- 1 can (14 oz.) sweetened condensed milk
- 1 pkg. (6 squares) BAKER'S White Chocolate, melted
- 2 tsp. vanilla, divided
- 4 eggs
- 1 can (21 oz.) cherry pie filling
- 1 cup thawed COOL WHIP Whipped Topping

## ▶ make it!

1. **HEAT** oven to 300°F if using a silver 9-inch springform pan (or to 275°F if using a dark nonstick 9-inch springform pan).

2. **RESERVE** 16 of the pecan halves. Finely chop remaining pecans; mix with graham crumbs, sugar and margarine. Press firmly onto bottom of pan.

3. **BEAT** cream cheese in large bowl with electric mixer on medium speed until creamy. Gradually add sweetened condensed milk, beating until well blended. Add chocolate and 1 tsp. of the vanilla; mix well. Add eggs, 1 at a time, mixing on low speed just until blended. Pour over crust.

4. **BAKE** 1 hour or until center is almost set. Run knife around rim of pan to loosen cake; cool before removing rim. Refrigerate 4 hours or overnight.

5. **MIX** pie filling and remaining vanilla; spoon over cheesecake. Top with COOL WHIP and reserved pecan halves.

# PHILADELPHIA blueberry crown cheesecake

**PREP: 15 min. | TOTAL: 5 hours 15 min. | MAKES: 16 servings.**

## ▶ what you need!

30 NILLA Wafers, crushed (about 1 cup)

1 cup plus 3 Tbsp. sugar, divided

3 Tbsp. butter or margarine, melted

5 pkg. (8 oz. each) PHILADELPHIA Cream Cheese, softened

3 Tbsp. flour

1 Tbsp. vanilla

Grated zest from 1 medium lemon

1 cup BREAKSTONE'S or KNUDSEN Sour Cream

4 eggs

2 cups fresh blueberries

## ▶ make it!

1. **HEAT** oven to 325°F.

2. **MIX** wafer crumbs, 3 Tbsp. of the sugar and butter until well blended. Press firmly onto bottom of 9-inch springform pan.

3. **BEAT** cream cheese, remaining 1 cup sugar, flour, vanilla and lemon zest with electric mixer on medium speed until well blended. Add sour cream; mix well. Add eggs, 1 at a time, beating on low speed after each addition just until blended. Pour over crust; top with blueberries.

4. **BAKE** 1 hour 10 min. to 1 hour 15 min. or until center is almost set. Run small knife or spatula around rim of pan to loosen cake; cool before removing rim of pan. Refrigerate at least 4 hours before serving. Store leftover cheesecake in refrigerator.

**SIZE IT UP:**
Savor a serving of this crowd-pleasing dessert on special occasions.

**SPECIAL EXTRA:**
Garnish with additional blueberries and fresh mint sprigs just before serving.

**GREAT SUBSTITUTE:**
Substitute 1 bag (16 oz.) thawed frozen blueberries or 1 can (15 oz.) blueberries, well drained, for the 2 cups fresh blueberries.

# Cakes, Pies & More

Time-tested cakes, no-bake desserts, pies, bars, cupcakes, and brownies for every occasion

# warm & gooey peanut butter-chocolate cake

**PREP: 15 min. | TOTAL: 45 min. | MAKES: 16 servings.**

## ▶ what you need!

1 pkg. (2-layer size) chocolate cake mix

½ cup butter, melted

4 eggs, divided

1 pkg. (8 oz.) PHILADELPHIA Cream Cheese, softened

½ cup creamy peanut butter

2 cups powdered sugar

## ▶ make it!

1. **HEAT** oven to 350°F.

2. **BEAT** cake mix, butter and 2 eggs with mixer on low speed 30 sec., stopping frequently to scrape beater and side of bowl. Beat on medium speed 2 min. Spread onto bottom of 13×9-inch pan sprayed with cooking spray.

3. **BEAT** remaining ingredients until well blended; pour over batter in pan.

4. **BAKE** 30 min. or until edges are firm. Cool slightly.

**SIZE WISE:**
Since this indulgent cake makes 16 servings, it's the perfect dessert to serve at your next party.

**KEEPING IT SAFE:**
Refrigerate any leftovers.

**SUBSTITUTE:**
Swap in your favorite flavor of cake mix to change up the flavor.

# BAKER'S one bowl cream cheese brownies

**PREP: 15 min. | TOTAL: 55 min. | MAKES: 32 servings.**

## ▶ what you need!

4 squares BAKER'S Unsweetened Chocolate

¾ cup butter

2½ cups sugar, divided

5 eggs, divided

1¼ cups flour, divided

1 pkg. (8 oz.) PHILADELPHIA Cream Cheese, softened

## ▶ make it!

1. **HEAT** oven to 350°F.

2. **LINE** 13×9-inch pan with foil, with ends of foil extending over sides. Grease foil.

3. **MICROWAVE** chocolate and butter in large microwaveable bowl on HIGH 2 min. or until butter is melted. Stir until chocolate is completely melted. Add 2 cups sugar; stir until well blended. Add 4 eggs; mix well. Stir in 1 cup flour until well blended; spread into prepared pan.

4. **BEAT** cream cheese and remaining sugar, egg and flour in same bowl with whisk until well blended. Spoon over brownie batter; swirl gently with knife.

5. **BAKE** 35 to 40 min. or until toothpick inserted in center comes out with fudgy crumbs. (Do not overbake.) Cool completely. Use foil handles to lift brownies from pan before cutting to serve.

**BAKING IN GLASS BAKING DISH:**
If a recipe calls for a metal pan and you substitute a glass baking dish, always reduce the oven temperature by 25°F. This is necessary since the glass dish conducts and retains heat better than the metal pan.

# banana split "cake"

PREP: 15 min. | TOTAL: 5 hours 15 min. | MAKES: 24 servings.

## ► what you need!

9 HONEY MAID Honey Grahams, crushed (about 1½ cups)

1 cup sugar, divided

⅓ cup butter, melted

2 pkg. (8 oz. each) PHILADELPHIA Cream Cheese, softened

1 can (20 oz.) DOLE Crushed Pineapple, in juice, drained

6 bananas, divided

2 pkg. (3.4 oz. each) JELL-O Vanilla Flavor Instant Pudding

2 cups cold milk

2 cups thawed COOL WHIP Whipped Topping, divided

1 cup PLANTERS Chopped Pecans

## ► make it!

1. **MIX** graham crumbs, ¼ cup sugar and butter; press onto bottom of 13×9-inch pan. Freeze 10 min.

2. **BEAT** cream cheese and remaining sugar with mixer until well blended. Spread carefully over crust; top with pineapple. Slice 4 bananas; arrange over pineapple.

3. **BEAT** dry pudding mixes and milk with whisk 2 min. until well blended. Stir in 1 cup COOL WHIP; spread over banana layer in pan. Top with remaining COOL WHIP. Refrigerate 5 hours. Slice remaining 2 bananas just before serving; arrange over dessert. Top with nuts.

**SIZE-WISE:**
This banana split-inspired dessert makes a great treat to share with friends and family.

**SHORTCUT:**
Substitute 1½ cups HONEY MAID Graham Cracker Crumbs for the crushed grahams.

# caramel apple dessert

**PREP: 15 min. | TOTAL: 5 hours 15 min. | MAKES: 16 servings.**

## ▶ what you need!

60  NILLA Wafers, finely crushed (about 2 cups)

⅓  cup butter, melted

1  pkg. (8 oz.) PHILADELPHIA Cream Cheese, softened

¼  cup sugar

3¼  cups milk, divided

1  tub (8 oz.) COOL WHIP Whipped Topping, thawed, divided

2  pkg. (3.4 oz. each) JELL-O Vanilla Flavor Instant Pudding

½  cup caramel ice cream topping, divided

1  each red and green apple, chopped

¼  cup PLANTERS COCKTAIL Peanuts, chopped

## ▶ make it!

1. **MIX** wafer crumbs and butter; press onto bottom of 13×9-inch pan. Beat cream cheese, sugar and ¼ cup milk with mixer until well blended. Stir in 1 cup COOL WHIP; spread over crust.

2. **BEAT** dry pudding mixes and remaining milk with whisk 2 min. Stir in ¼ cup caramel topping.

3. **SPOON** over cream cheese layer; top with remaining COOL WHIP.

4. **REFRIGERATE** 5 hours or until firm. Top with apples, nuts and remaining caramel topping just before serving.

**KEEP APPLES FROM TURNING BROWN:**
After cutting the apples, minimize browning by dipping them in 1 cup water mixed with 1 Tbsp. lemon juice before adding to dessert.

# cappuccino bars

PREP: 10 min. | TOTAL: 3 hours 10 min. | MAKES: 32 servings, 1 bar each.

## ▶ what you need!

15 HONEY MAID Honey Grahams

2 pkg. (8 oz. each) PHILADELPHIA Cream Cheese, softened

3½ cups cold milk, divided

3 pkg. (3.9 oz. each) JELL-O Chocolate Instant Pudding

1 Tbsp. MAXWELL HOUSE Instant Coffee

¼ tsp. ground cinnamon

1 tub (8 oz.) COOL WHIP Whipped Topping, thawed, divided

1 square BAKER'S Semi-Sweet Chocolate, grated or 3 Tbsp. chocolate sprinkles

## ▶ make it!

1. **ARRANGE** half of the grahams in bottom of 13×9-inch pan, cutting grahams to fit if necessary.

2. **BEAT** cream cheese in large bowl with electric mixer on low speed until creamy. Gradually add 1 cup of the milk, beating until well blended. Add remaining 2½ cups milk, the dry pudding mixes, coffee granules and cinnamon. Beat 1 to 2 min. or until well blended. (Mixture will be thick.) Gently stir in 2 cups COOL WHIP.

3. **SPREAD** half of the pudding mixture over grahams in pan; arrange remaining grahams over pudding. Cover with remaining pudding mixture; top with remaining COOL WHIP. Sprinkle with grated chocolate. Freeze 3 hours or overnight. Cut into 32 bars to serve. Store leftover bars in freezer.

**SIZE WISE:**
Serve this easy frozen treat at your next celebration.

**HOW TO THAW COOL WHIP:**
Place unopened 8-oz. tub of COOL WHIP Whipped Topping in the refrigerator for 4 hours. Do not thaw in the microwave.

# CHIPS AHOY! house

PREP: 40 min. | TOTAL: 1 hour 10 min. | MAKES: 16 servings.

## ▶ what you need!

  2 pkg. (8 oz. each) PHILADELPHIA Cream Cheese, softened

  4 squares BAKER'S Semi-Sweet Chocolate, melted

  ¼ cup sugar

  1 tsp. vanilla

  ½ cup thawed COOL WHIP Whipped Topping

  3 pkg. (10 oz. each) frozen pound cake, thawed

15 CHIPS AHOY! Candy Blasts Real Chocolate Chip Cookies

  5 chocolate-covered cookie sticks

10 candy-coated chocolate pieces

## ▶ make it!

1. **BEAT** cream cheese in large bowl with electric mixer until creamy. Add chocolate, sugar and vanilla; mix just until blended. Gently stir in COOL WHIP; cover. Refrigerate 30 min.

2. **TRIM** rounded tops off cakes. Place two of the cakes, side-by-side, on parchment-covered wire racks. Spread lightly with small amount of the cream cheese mixture. Stand remaining cake on one of the short ends; cut diagonally in half to make two triangles. Place triangles on iced cakes in shape of pyramid to resemble roof. Spread entire cake with remaining cream cheese mixture. Transfer cake to serving platter.

3. **PRESS** chocolate chip cookies onto roof to resemble roof tiles. Press chocolate-covered cookie sticks onto side of house for the door and top of house for the chimney. Decorate with chocolate pieces as desired. Store in refrigerator.

**SIZE-WISE:**
This delightful cake is fun to decorate but extremely indulgent, so enjoy it only on special occasions.

**FAMILY FUN:**
Make this a family project by decorating this edible house with the kids.

# chocolate-caramel creme pie

**PREP: 30 min. | TOTAL: 3 hours 30 min. | MAKES: 8 servings.**

## ▸ what you need!

18 OREO Cookies, finely crushed (about 1½ cups)

3 Tbsp. butter, melted

4 oz. (½ of 8-oz. pkg.) PHILADELPHIA Cream Cheese, softened

2 Tbsp. caramel ice cream topping

1 cup thawed COOL WHIP Whipped Topping

1 pkg. (3.9 oz.) JELL-O Chocolate Instant Pudding

1½ cups cold milk

## ▸ make it!

1. **COMBINE** cookie crumbs and butter; press onto bottom and up sides of 9-inch pie plate sprayed with cooking spray. Refrigerate until ready to use.

2. **MIX** cream cheese and caramel topping in medium bowl until well blended. Gently stir in COOL WHIP; spread onto bottom of crust.

3. **BEAT** dry pudding mix and milk with whisk 2 min.; pour over cream cheese layer. Refrigerate 3 hours.

# candy bar pie

**PREP: 20 min. | TOTAL: 4 hours 20 min. | MAKES: 10 servings.**

## ▶ what you need!

4 oz. (½ of 8-oz. pkg.) PHILADELPHIA Cream Cheese, softened

1 Tbsp. milk

1 tub (12 oz.) COOL WHIP Whipped Topping, thawed, divided

1 (2.07-oz.) chocolate-coated caramel-peanut nougat bar, finely chopped

2 pkg. (3.9 oz. each) JELL-O Chocolate Instant Pudding

1½ cups cold milk

1 OREO Pie Crust (6 oz.)

## ▶ make it!

1. **MIX** cream cheese and 1 Tbsp. milk in large bowl with whisk until well blended. Stir in 1½ cups COOL WHIP and candy; set aside.

2. **BEAT** dry pudding mixes and 1½ cups milk in separate large bowl with whisk 2 min. (Pudding will be thick.) Stir in the remaining COOL WHIP; spread half onto bottom of crust. Cover with layers of cream cheese mixture and remaining pudding mixture.

3. **REFRIGERATE** 4 hours or until firm. Garnish with remaining COOL WHIP before serving.

**HOW TO SOFTEN CREAM CHEESE:**
Place measured amount of cream cheese in microwaveable bowl. Microwave on HIGH 10 sec. or until slightly softened.

# coffee-drizzled cream cheese pie

**PREP: 15 min. | TOTAL: 2 hours 15 min. | MAKES: 8 servings.**

## ▶ what you need!

1 pkg. (8 oz.) PHILADELPHIA Cream Cheese, softened

⅓ cup sugar

½ cup milk

2 Tbsp. GENERAL FOODS INTERNATIONAL Suisse Mocha Café

1 HONEY MAID Graham Pie Crust (6 oz.)

1 tub (8 oz.) COOL WHIP Whipped Topping, thawed

## ▶ make it!

1. **BEAT** cream cheese in medium bowl until creamy. Gradually add sugar, mixing until well blended. Stir in milk. Remove ¼ cup of the cream cheese mixture; place in small bowl. Stir in flavored instant coffee mix. Drizzle 1 Tbsp. of the coffee-flavored cream cheese mixture onto bottom of crust. Set remaining coffee-flavored cream cheese mixture aside.

2. **STIR** COOL WHIP gently into remaining plain cream cheese mixture, stirring just until combined. Spoon into crust. Drizzle with remaining coffee-flavored cream cheese mixture. Swirl knife gently through mixtures several times for marble effect.

3. **REFRIGERATE** 2 hours or until set. Store leftover pie in refrigerator.

**SIZE IT UP:**
Desserts can be part of a balanced diet, but remember to keep tabs on portions.

**GREAT SUBSTITUTE:**
Omit milk. Substitute 1 cup BREAKSTONE'S or KNUDSEN Sour Cream for the cream cheese.

# cookies & cream freeze

## ▶ what you need!

- 4  squares BAKER'S Semi-Sweet Chocolate
- 14  OREO Cookies, divided
- 1  pkg. (8 oz.) PHILADELPHIA Cream Cheese, softened
- ¼  cup sugar
- ½  tsp. vanilla
- 1  tub (8 oz.) COOL WHIP Whipped Topping, thawed

## ▶ make it!

1. **MELT** chocolate as directed on package; set aside until ready to use. Line 8½×4½-inch loaf pan with foil, with ends of foil extending over sides of pan. Arrange 8 of the cookies evenly on bottom of pan. Crumble remaining 6 cookies; set aside.

2. **BEAT** cream cheese, sugar and vanilla in medium bowl with electric mixer until well blended. Stir in COOL WHIP. Remove about 1½ cups of the cream cheese mixture; place in medium bowl. Stir in melted chocolate.

3. **SPREAD** remaining cream cheese mixture over cookies in pan; sprinkle with crumbled cookies. Gently press cookies into cream cheese mixture with back of spoon; top with chocolate mixture. Cover. Freeze 3 hours or until firm. Remove from freezer about 15 min. before serving; invert onto serving plate. Peel off foil; let stand at room temperature to soften slightly before cutting to serve.

**SPECIAL EXTRA:**
Drizzle serving plates with additional melted BAKER'S Semi-Sweet Chocolate for a spectacular, yet simple, dessert presentation.

**SIZE WISE:**
Sweets can be part of a balanced diet but remember to keep tabs on portions.

# cream cheese flan

**PREP: 20 min. | TOTAL: 4 hours 20 min. | MAKES: 8 servings.**

## ▶ what you need!

2 cups sugar, divided

1 can (12 oz.) evaporated milk

1 pkg. (8 oz.) PHILADELPHIA Cream Cheese, cubed, softened

5 eggs

1 tsp. vanilla

Dash salt

## ▶ make it!

1. **HEAT** oven to 350°F.

2. **COOK** 1 cup sugar in small heavy saucepan on medium heat until sugar is melted and deep golden brown, stirring constantly. Pour into 9-inch round pan; tilt pan to evenly cover bottom with syrup.

3. **BLEND** evaporated milk and cream cheese in blender until smooth. Add remaining sugar, eggs, vanilla and salt; blend just until smooth. Pour over syrup in pan. Place filled pan in larger pan; add enough hot water to larger pan to come halfway up side of smaller pan.

4. **BAKE** 50 min. to 1 hour or until knife inserted near center comes out clean. Cool slightly. Carefully remove flan from water. Cool completely on wire rack. Refrigerate several hours or until chilled. Unmold onto plate just before serving. Garnish as desired.

**HOW TO UNMOLD FLAN:**
Bake and refrigerate flan as directed. Run metal knife around edge of flan. Invert onto plate; shake gently to loosen. Gently twist to remove pan. To soften any remaining caramel in pan, dip bottom of pan in hot water; spoon caramel over flan.

**FLAVOR VARIATIONS:**
**Guava:** Add ½ cup guava paste, cut into pieces, or ½ cup canned guava shells in heavy syrup to cream cheese batter before pouring into prepared pan. **Lime:** Add zest from 1 lime to boiling sugar mixture; remove from syrup before sugar caramelizes. Pour into prepared pan as directed. **Cajeta:** Add ¼ cup cajeta (Mexican goat milk caramel) to cream cheese batter before pouring into prepared pan. **Chocolate-Orange:** Add 2 squares BAKER'S Semi-Sweet Chocolate, melted and cooled, and 1 Tbsp. orange zest to cream cheese batter before pouring into prepared pan. **Coconut:** Omit vanilla and add ¼ cup BAKER'S ANGEL FLAKE Coconut or ½ cup coconut milk and 1 Tbsp. rum to cream cheese batter before pouring into prepared pan.

# layered strawberry cheesecake bowl

**PREP: 20 min. | TOTAL: 4 hours 20 min. | MAKES: 14 servings, ⅔ cup each.**

## ▶ what you need!

3 cups sliced fresh strawberries

3 Tbsp. sugar

2 pkg. (8 oz. each) PHILADELPHIA Neufchâtel Cheese, softened

1½ cups cold milk

1 pkg. (3.4 oz.) JELL-O Vanilla Flavor Instant Pudding

2 cups thawed COOL WHIP LITE Whipped Topping, divided

2 cups frozen pound cake cubes (1 inch)

1 square BAKER'S Semi-Sweet Chocolate

## ▶ make it!

1. **COMBINE** berries and sugar; refrigerate until ready to use. Beat Neufchâtel with mixer until creamy. Gradually beat in milk. Add dry pudding mix; mix well.

2. **BLEND** in 1½ cups COOL WHIP. Spoon half into 2½-qt. bowl.

3. **TOP** with layers of cake, berries and remaining Neufchâtel mixture. Refrigerate 4 hours.

4. **MELT** chocolate; drizzle over trifle. Top with remaining COOL WHIP.

**SPECIAL EXTRA:**
Garnish with a chocolate-covered strawberry just before serving.

**NOTE:**
You will need about half of a 10.75-oz. package pound cake to get the 2 cups cake cubes needed to prepare this recipe.

**SIZE-WISE:**
Enjoy your favorite foods while keeping portion size in mind.

# lemon tropical pound cake

**PREP: 20 min. | TOTAL: 1 hour 50 min. | MAKES: 12 servings.**

## ▶ what you need!

1 pkg. (8 oz.) PHILADELPHIA Cream Cheese, softened

½ cup butter or margarine, softened

1½ cups granulated sugar

4 eggs

2 cups flour

1½ tsp. CALUMET Baking Powder

1 pkg. (3 oz.) JELL-O Lemon Flavor Gelatin

1½ cups chopped dried fruit (mango, papaya and pineapple), divided

1 cup PLANTERS Chopped Pecans, divided

1 cup powdered sugar

2 Tbsp. lemon juice

## ▶ make it!

1. **HEAT** oven to 350°F.

2. **BEAT** cream cheese, butter and granulated sugar in large bowl with electric mixer on medium speed until well blended. Add eggs, 1 at a time, mixing well after each addition. Gradually add flour, baking powder and dry gelatin mix, mixing on low speed until well blended. Stir in 1 cup of the dried fruit and ½ cup nuts. Pour into greased parchment paper-lined 9-inch square baking pan.

3. **BAKE** 1 hour or until toothpick inserted in center comes out clean and cake is golden brown. Cool 5 min. Invert cake onto wire rack; remove pan. Cool completely.

4. **MIX** powdered sugar and lemon juice; spread over top and sides of cake. Top cake with remaining ½ cup dried fruit and ½ cup nuts.

**SIZE-WISE:**
You'll know it's a special occasion when you enjoy a serving of this cake.

**SUBSTITUTE:**
You can substitute a slightly larger size pan for the one called for in the recipe. Try using a 12-cup fluted or 10-inch tube pan, or a 9- or 10-inch round cake pan at least 2 inches deep. Do not use a smaller pan or the batter may run over the top of the pan during baking. Remember that a different pan size affects the baking time (a larger pan may shorten baking times), so check for doneness earlier than the recipe specifies.

# pumpkin cream cupcakes

**PREP: 10 min. | TOTAL: 31 min. | MAKES: 24 servings, 1 cupcake each.**

## ▶ what you need!

1 pkg. (2-layer size) spice cake mix

1 pkg. (3.4 oz.) JELL-O Vanilla Flavor Instant Pudding

1 cup canned pumpkin

1 pkg. (8 oz.) PHILADELPHIA Cream Cheese, softened

¼ cup sugar

1 egg

## ▶ make it!

1. **HEAT** oven to 350°F.

2. **PREPARE** cake batter as directed on package. Add dry pudding mix and pumpkin; mix well. Spoon into 24 paper-lined muffin cups.

3. **BEAT** cream cheese with mixer until creamy. Blend in sugar and egg; spoon over batter.

4. **BAKE** 18 to 21 min. or until toothpick inserted in centers comes out clean. Cool 5 min.; remove to wire racks. Cool completely.

**SPECIAL EXTRA:**
Stir ¼ tsp. ground nutmeg into 1½ cups thawed COOL WHIP Whipped Topping; spread over cooled cupcakes. Keep refrigerated.

# walnut-praline cake with cream cheese frosting

**PREP: 30 min. | TOTAL: 1 hour 55 min. | MAKES: 16 servings, 1 slice each.**

## ▶ what you need!

1 pkg. (6 oz.) PLANTERS Walnut Pieces, divided

1 pkg. (2-layer size) white cake mix

½ cup granulated sugar

2 Tbsp. water

1 pkg. (8 oz.) PHILADELPHIA Cream Cheese, softened

½ cup butter, softened

1 pkg. (16 oz.) powdered sugar

3 squares BAKER'S Bittersweet Chocolate, divided

## ▶ make it!

1. **HEAT** oven to 350°F.

2. **GREASE** and flour 2 (9-inch) round baking pans. Process ⅔ cup nuts in food processor or blender until finely ground; set aside. Prepare cake batter as directed on package. Stir in ground nuts. Pour evenly into prepared pans. Bake 25 min. or until wooden toothpick inserted in centers comes out clean. Cool cake layers in pans 10 min. on wire racks. Remove cakes from pans; cool completely.

3. **MEANWHILE,** cover baking sheet with foil; spray with cooking spray. Mix granulated sugar and water in small saucepan. Bring to boil on medium-high heat. Reduce heat to medium-low; simmer 5 min. or until deep golden brown, stirring occasionally. Stir in remaining nuts; spread onto prepared baking sheet. Cool completely. Carefully remove nuts from foil; break into small clusters.

4. **BEAT** cream cheese and butter in large bowl with electric mixer on medium speed until well blended. Gradually add powdered sugar, beating well after each addition. Remove 2 cups of the frosting; set aside. Melt chocolate as directed on package; cool slightly. Add two-thirds of the chocolate to remaining frosting in bowl; beat until well blended.

5. **CUT** each cake layer horizontally into 2 layers. Stack cake layers on serving plate, spreading chocolate frosting between layers. Frost top and sides of cake with reserved plain cream cheese frosting. Gently press nut clusters into top of cake. Drizzle with remaining melted chocolate. Store in refrigerator.

**MAKE AHEAD:**
Cake layers, walnut praline and cream cheese frosting can be made 1 day ahead. Keep cake layers covered at room temperature; store praline in airtight container at room temperature. Refrigerate frosting until ready to use; soften before spreading over cake.

**SUBSTITUTE:**
Substitute PLANTERS Slivered Almonds or Pecan Pieces for the walnuts.

**PRALINE COATING COOKING TIP:**
After mixing sugar and water in saucepan, brush down side of saucepan with a clean wet pastry brush. This will help prevent the sugar from caramelizing on the side of the pan. For best results, continue to brush down side of saucepan as needed with clean wet brush to ensure even cooking of the praline coating.

# raspberry kisses

**PREP: 10 min. | TOTAL: 10 min. | MAKES: 2 doz. or 12 servings, 2 cookie sandwiches each.**

## ▶ what you need!

48  NILLA Wafers

½  cup (½ of 8-oz. tub) PHILADELPHIA Cream Cheese Spread

¼  cup seedless raspberry jam or preserves

1  Tbsp. powdered sugar

## ▶ make it!

1. **SPREAD** 24 wafers each with 1 tsp. cream cheese spread; top each with ½ tsp. jam.

2. **COVER** with remaining wafers to make sandwiches.

3. **SPRINKLE** with sugar.

**VARIATION:**
Prepare using Reduced Fat NILLA Wafers and PHILADELPHIA Neufchâtel Cheese.

**NOTE:**
For crisper texture, serve immediately. Or for a cake-like texture, place in airtight container and store in refrigerator overnight before serving.

**NOTE:**
Store leftovers in airtight container in refrigerator.

# peanut butter &
# fudge swirl pie

**PREP: 15 min. | TOTAL: 4 hours 15 min. | MAKES: 8 servings.**

## ▶ what you need!

1 pkg. (8 oz.) PHILADELPHIA Cream Cheese, softened

½ cup sugar

¼ cup creamy peanut butter

2 cups thawed COOL WHIP Whipped Topping

1 OREO Pie Crust (6 oz.)

¼ cup hot fudge ice cream topping, warmed

## ▶ make it!

1. **BEAT** cream cheese, sugar and peanut butter in large bowl with mixer until well blended. Whisk in COOL WHIP.

2. **SPOON** into crust. Drizzle with fudge topping; swirl gently with knife.

3. **REFRIGERATE** 4 hours or until firm.

**SPECIAL EXTRA:**
Garnish with 2 Tbsp. chopped PLANTERS COCKTAIL Peanuts.

# triple-chocolate mousse cake

**PREP: 25 min. | TOTAL: 4 hours 55 min. | MAKES: 24 servings.**

## ▶ what you need!

½ cup chocolate syrup

1 pkg. (2-layer size) chocolate cake mix

1 cup water

⅓ cup oil

7 eggs, divided

½ cup BREAKSTONE'S or KNUDSEN Sour Cream

1 pkg. (8 oz.) PHILADELPHIA Cream Cheese, softened

1 cup sugar

1 can (12 oz.) evaporated milk

4 squares BAKER'S Semi-Sweet Chocolate, melted

1 cup thawed COOL WHIP Whipped Topping

## ▶ make it!

1. **HEAT** oven to 375°F.

2. **SPRAY** 12-cup fluted tube pan with cooking spray; pour in chocolate syrup.

3. **BEAT** cake mix, water, oil and 3 eggs with mixer 2 min. or until well blended; blend in sour cream. Pour over syrup in pan.

4. **BEAT** cream cheese and sugar with mixer until well blended. Add remaining eggs; mix well. Blend in evaporated milk and melted chocolate; gently spoon over cake batter in pan. Cover with foil sprayed with cooking spray, sprayed-side down.

5. **PLACE** tube pan in shallow pan. Add enough water to larger pan to come at least 2 inches up side of tube pan. Bake 1 hour 30 min. or until toothpick inserted near center comes out clean. Cool completely in pan on wire rack. Refrigerate 2 hours. Invert cake onto plate; remove pan. Serve cake with COOL WHIP.

**SIZE-WISE:**
Since this layered chocolate cake makes 24 servings, it's the perfect dessert to serve at your next party.

**NOTE:**
The cream cheese mixture sinks to the bottom of the cake batter in pan as the cake bakes, forming the mousse layer at the top of the unmolded cake. To unmold cooled cake, use long thin spatula to loosen cake from side of pan. Place plate over cake pan; invert cake onto plate. Gently remove pan. Spoon any chocolate syrup remaining in pan over cake.

**IMPORTANT NOTE:**
To prevent overflow, check cake pan to confirm it's the required 12-cup size. Just measure 3 qt. (12 cups) water and pour into empty pan to verify the volume before using as directed. If you only have a 10-cup fluted tube pan, reserve 2 cups cake batter before pouring remaining batter into prepared tube pan. Continue as directed. Reserved cake batter will make 9 cupcakes. Bake as directed on cake mix package.

# white chocolate-raspberry cheesecake bars

**PREP: 20 min. | TOTAL: 4 hours 53 min. | MAKES: 9 servings.**

## ▶ what you need!

12  OREO Cookies, finely crushed (about 1 cup)

2  Tbsp. butter, melted

3  squares BAKER'S White Chocolate, divided

2  pkg. (8 oz. each) PHILADELPHIA Cream Cheese, softened

½  cup sugar

1  tsp. vanilla

2  eggs

¼  cup red raspberry preserves

## ▶ make it!

1. **HEAT** oven to 350°F.

2. **MIX** cookie crumbs and butter; press onto bottom of 8- or 9-inch square pan. Melt 2 chocolate squares as directed on package.

3. **BEAT** cream cheese, sugar and vanilla in large bowl with mixer until well blended. Add melted chocolate; mix well. Add eggs, 1 at a time, mixing on low speed after each just until blended. Pour over crust.

4. **BAKE** 25 to 28 min. or until center is almost set. Cool 5 min.; spread with preserves. Melt remaining chocolate square; drizzle over cheesecake. Cool cheesecake completely. Refrigerate 4 hours.

# Index

## R

## S

# METRIC CONVERSION CHART

## VOLUME MEASUREMENTS (dry)

1/8 teaspoon = 0.5 mL
1/4 teaspoon = 1 mL
1/2 teaspoon = 2 mL
3/4 teaspoon = 4 mL
1 teaspoon = 5 mL
1 tablespoon = 15 mL
2 tablespoons = 30 mL
1/4 cup = 60 mL
1/3 cup = 75 mL
1/2 cup = 125 mL
2/3 cup = 150 mL
3/4 cup = 175 mL
1 cup = 250 mL
2 cups = 1 pint = 500 mL
3 cups = 750 mL
4 cups = 1 quart = 1 L

## VOLUME MEASUREMENTS (fluid)

1 fluid ounce (2 tablespoons) = 30 mL
4 fluid ounces (1/2 cup) = 125 mL
8 fluid ounces (1 cup) = 250 mL
12 fluid ounces (1 1/2 cups) = 375 mL
16 fluid ounces (2 cups) = 500 mL

## WEIGHTS (mass)

1/2 ounce = 15 g
1 ounce = 30 g
3 ounces = 90 g
4 ounces = 120 g
8 ounces = 225 g
10 ounces = 285 g
12 ounces = 360 g
16 ounces = 1 pound = 450 g

## DIMENSIONS

1/16 inch = 2 mm
1/8 inch = 3 mm
1/4 inch = 6 mm
1/2 inch = 1.5 cm
3/4 inch = 2 cm
1 inch = 2.5 cm

## OVEN TEMPERATURES

250°F = 120°C
275°F = 140°C
300°F = 150°C
325°F = 160°C
350°F = 180°C
375°F = 190°C
400°F = 200°C
425°F = 220°C
450°F = 230°C

## BAKING PAN SIZES

| Utensil | Size in Inches/Quarts | Metric Volume | Size in Centimeters |
|---|---|---|---|
| Baking or Cake Pan (square or rectangular) | 8×8×2 | 2 L | 20×20×5 |
| | 9×9×2 | 2.5 L | 23×23×5 |
| | 12×8×2 | 3 L | 30×20×5 |
| | 13×9×2 | 3.5 L | 33×23×5 |
| Loaf Pan | 8×4×3 | 1.5 L | 20×10×7 |
| | 9×5×3 | 2 L | 23×13×7 |
| Round Layer Cake Pan | 8×1½ | 1.2 L | 20×4 |
| | 9×1½ | 1.5 L | 23×4 |
| Pie Plate | 8×1¼ | 750 mL | 20×3 |
| | 9×1¼ | 1 L | 23×3 |
| Baking Dish or Casserole | 1 quart | 1 L | — |
| | 1½ quarts | 1.5 L | — |
| | 2 quarts | 2 L | — |